The Life and Times of
RICHARD II

ENDPAPERS This crayon drawing (*c.* 1400) by Forestier shows London as it would have appeared during Richard II's reign.
OVERLEAF LEFT The National Gallery's portrait of Richard, by an unknown artist, is unusual in showing him wearing a moustache.

RIGHT Richard adopted his mother's emblem of the white hart, shown here as it appears on the back of the *Wilton Diptych*, and it became the insignia of his retainers.

ICARDVS
II

The Life and Times of

RICHARD II

Michael Senior

Introduction by Antonia Fraser

Weidenfeld and Nicolson
London

First produced in 1981 by George Weidenfeld and Nicolson Limited 91 Clapham High Street London SW4 7TA

Picture research by Christine Vincent
Layout by Sheila Sherwen

Filmset by Keyspools Limited, Golborne, Lancashire
Printed in Great Britain by Morrison and Gibb, Edinburgh

Contents

Introduction

'A WONDERFUL LAND is this, and a fickle; which hath exiled, slain, destroyed or ruined so many Kings, rulers and great men, and is ever tainted with strife and variance and envy': so said Richard II in 1399, at his enforced abdication from the throne of England in favour of his cousin Bolingbroke – the future Henry IV. The ex-king was left in the Tower of London 'musing on his ancient and wonted glory and on the fickle fortune of the world'.

These are the actual words, spoken by the thirty-two year old monarch 'sorrowfully' and recorded by Adam of Usk. But most of us will think of the deposition of Richard II in terms of one of Shakespeare's greatest speeches (which clearly derives its inspiration from Adam of Usk's firsthand report). Indeed, so indelibly is Shakespeare's character of Richard II stamped on our imagination – as, in a different way, is his Richard III – that it is fortunate he was able to draw upon such reliable sources. In consequence, as Michael Senior demonstrates in this lucid biographical study, Shakespeare's portrait of Richard II is not only an artistic masterpiece, but is also remarkably accurate historically.

Richard Plantagenet, son of the martial Black Prince and Joan, the Fair Maid of Kent, was born in 1367; he succeeded his grandfather Edward III ten years later. His sumptuous yet hurried coronation indicated the cracking structure of the country at the time, which his uncle John of Gaunt, as *de facto* ruler, was concerned to shore up. This was a land haunted on the one hand by the spectre of the past – the Black Death, that nightmare visitation of bubonic plague which had carried away as much as thirty per cent of the population – and on the other hand by unrest in the future from all levels of society.

The great magnates surrounded the throne: the perennially vexed question of the succession finally erupted into the quarrel of York and Lancaster in the next century. Lower down the social scale, discontent culminated in the Peasants' Revolt of 1381 in which Richard displayed considerable personal courage, if also an ability for double-dealing, later to be held against him. The aptly named Merciless Parliament of 1387 showed that no subservience could be taken for granted from the comparatively new parliamentary assembly.

The most generally accepted artistic image of Richard II,

from the Wilton Diptych, shows the fragile look of a medieval beauty; with his first wife, the beloved Anne of Bohemia, Richard presided over a court remarkable for its refinement and its European cultural links. The king's patronage extended to Chaucer – his Clerk of the Works – and Westminster Hall still provides today an architectural memorial to his reign. Yet Richard II was born to a constitutional crisis which he could not, and did not, solve; it remained to plague his successors. The tortuous interplay of Richard's own character with the problems of 'strife and variance and envy' which faced him is here masterfully delineated.

Antonia Fraser

Acknowledgements

Photographs and illustrations are supplied or reproduced by kind permission of the following: Abbey of St Denis, Paris, 131 (photography by Godfrey New); Bibliotèque National, Paris, 10–11, 28, 32, 34–5, 96 above (Robert Harding Associates), 120–1, 161 above and below (Robert Harding Associates); Bodleian Library, Oxford, 36 below, 54 below right, 56, 80 below (Angela Murphy), 81 above, centre and below (Angela Murphy), 92, 96 below (Arthur Lockwood), 97, 105 above and below, 138; British Museum, London, 13 (Fotomas Index), 14–15, 16 above and below, 17 above and below (Arthur Lockwood), 18 (Arthur Lockwood), 29, 30, 33, 38–9 (Ikon), 45, 47, 48–9, 50–1 (Ikon), 54 above (Ikon), 57 above, 57 below (Arthur Lockwood), 60–1, 66–7, 68–9 (Ikon), 73, 74, 78–9, 80 above right, 84, 86–7, 89 (Ikon), 95, 96 centre (Arthur Lockwood), 106 left and right (Fotomas Index), 107 left and right (Fotomas Index), 111, 112 (Robert Harding Associates), 114 (Robert Harding Associates), 116, 134–5, 142, 153, 156–7, 165 (Ikon), 166 (Ikon), 168, 170–1, 174–5, 177, 179, 180–1 (Cooper-Bridgeman Library), 182–3, 185 (Cooper-Bridgeman Library), 186, 188–9, 191, 192, 194, 196, 198–9; Cambridge University Collection 25 below, 139 above and below; Cooper-Bridgeman Library, London, 104; Mary Evans Picture Library, London, 141; Fotomas Index, London, 19, 36 above; Giraudon, Paris, 25 above; Ikon, London, 159; Inner Temple, London, 124–5 left, centre and right (photography by Godfrey New); A. F. Kersting, London, 42, 91, 99; Museum of London endpapers; National Gallery, London, 3, 100–1; National Monuments Record 214; National Portrait Gallery, London, 21, 71; Michael Senior 187 above and below; Sidney Sussex College, Cambridge, 150 (Ikon); York Minster, Dean and Chapter, 200–1; Weidenfeld Archives, London, 23, 24 below, 41, 54 below left, 64, 80 above left, 128 left and right, 144, 145, 148, 154, 208–9, 213; Westminster Abbey, London, Dean and Chapter, 108 (Cooper-Bridgeman Library); Reg Wilson, London, 204, 205.

1 Times of Change

> The King passing the water rode a foure miles before hee came to the rocke; when he saw the ambushes he was sore abashed, knowing well he was betrayed by the Earle, for he was in such a place as hee could not escape. The sea beating on the one side and the rocke keeping him on the other, and if he should have fled backe, they would have caught him. . . .

So Stow's *Annals* tells us of the downfall of one of England's more intriguing kings. He was the last of the Plantagenets. His fall brought to an end the longest dynasty in our history so far, a formal succession of eight monarchs spanning two hundred and forty-five years. It led to Britain's most turbulent and disordered period, the struggle of the Houses of York and Lancaster, which ended, eighty-five years after his death, only with the arrival of a new royal line in the person of Henry Tudor, victorious on the battlefield of Bosworth. The story of how Richard came to find himself ambushed under that cliff is itself a part of England's social history and political growth. At times touching, at others exciting, it inevitably centres on the person of the king.

We are all whatever we are as a result both of our surrounding circumstances and of our individual temper and ability. This is as true of kings, and moreover the combination is highlighted by the effects which it has on all their dealings. Richard owed much of his make-up to history, and he gave back to history accordingly. With this monarch, however, as with few others, we are seldom able to forget that he was also a human being.

PREVIOUS PAGE The Battle of Poitiers, from the Bibliothèque Nationale, Paris; this was a major victory for the Black Prince, Richard's father. The French king was captured and held to ransom, the English territories in France were secured, and the Black Prince ruled Aquitaine from his court at Bordeaux, where Richard was born.

Richard was born into the heroic military world of the Hundred Years War, in which his father, the Black Prince, and his grandfather, Edward III, had distinguished themselves at battles such as Crécy and Poitiers. His time, however, was to be one mainly of peace, and his temperament favoured a style of life very different from that of his parents and ancestors. But although Richard did not go to war, he faced personal challenges in the form of conspiracy and insurrection throughout his reign, and he brought to bear on these the courage and even rashness which he had inherited from the Plantagenets. He became king at the age of ten, and as a boy of only fourteen he had to face one of the most traumatic of

An illustration from a copy of Chaucer's *Canterbury Tales* showing the life of a farmer in the fourteenth century. The open fields were cultivated in strips.

Britain's social upheavals, the Peasants' Revolt. In moments of crisis he showed monarchic qualities, but there were underlying weaknesses inherent both in his temperament and in his style of governing; and when the final confrontation with Bolingbroke came he failed to realize the weakness of his position.

In the meantime Richard's personal tastes and interests had done much to stimulate an English cultural reawakening.

Civilization was to be checked in its rapid advance by the long turmoil of the Wars of the Roses. One cannot help feeling that had Richard not been deposed, the English Renaissance would have come sooner than it did.

We have to imagine a country very different from our own. England in the fourteenth century was undergoing one of its periodic phases of recognizable change, but it was still closer to the simple early medieval structure than to the complicated land we know today. Both the look of the land and the way of life must have reflected this, and the strong current of economic and social change which we can identify so easily with hindsight was probably not so obvious to those who lived then, either at court or in the villages.

Feudalism was in decline, but it had set a pattern of land ownership and occupancy which was to underlie all future ones. Originating at the end of the Roman Empire, it had become

From a psalter of the 1340s, this scene shows the people of an East Anglian town doing the traditional round dance.

an established system of French society in the time of Charlemagne, was introduced to England by William the Conqueror, and had settled down into a comfortably effective agricultural and social form. Basically it had been a military as well as a land-owning system, by which vassals could enjoy the protection of a lord on the condition of granting him their aid in war. A tendency towards wage-earning rather than service had been initiated by the Crown itself with the institution of a paid army. When this replaced the levy of military service a major assumption of feudalism had been undermined. The same pattern was followed on the land: increasingly during the late thirteenth century it became the custom for a peasant, formerly bound to his lord as a 'villein' by an agreement of service, to commute this service to rent, and thus become the historical ancestor of our present tenant farmer. The system was further weakened by the dying out of the great and dominant Norman families, which in itself made feudal baronage a thing of the

Scenes from rural life

These illustrations from an early fourteenth-century manuscript show the seasonal tasks of medieval life.
TOP Scything grass
BOTTOM Beating down acorns to feed the swine

TOP Grape treading
BOTTOM Netting fish

Meat and poultry are chopped and prepared in the kitchen, before being taken to the table in small bowls. Cooking was elaborate and food was highly spiced.

past. In 1290 the formal death of feudalism was signalled by the Statute of *Quia Emptores*, which abolished subinfeudation.

All this gave rise to a slow but radical change in both the physical surroundings and the way of life in England, which makes Richard's reign a turning point in the development of the country's social history. The manor unit itself, with its open-field system of strip cultivation, was beginning to break down. Crofts with enclosed compounds dotted the surroundings of the 'great fields', which themselves were in fact not strictly open but protected against cattle by a large ditch or hedge. When a cataclysmic change struck Europe and England in the middle of the century the tendency to enclose, to move from cultivation to grazing, was suddenly accelerated. But even before that it can be assumed that the manorial farming unit was becoming increasingly complex.

At the same time another pre-existing trend was on the increase: the growth of towns. Together with this came a new range of social categories, and with that – significantly for

The lord and lady dine in the castle, while a servant attends to a beggar at the door. Patronage of the poor and sick was a traditional element of the medieval economy.

Richard's reign and role – a new spirit of freedom. There was as yet no squirearchy; this was to come into existence in Tudor times as the result of the amalgamation of holdings by increasingly prosperous tenant farmers, who were then able to purchase their lands from absentee and multiple owners. That side of the issue had already started. The holding of multiple manors by great lords gave rise, during our period, to a new degree of village independence. As some of these villages turned into small towns two new social classes – familiar enough as concepts to us now – came into being. The better paid craftsmen and particularly the more powerful urban guildsmen became a middle class. At the same time, and partly by occupying an intentionally exclusive position, they created below them the proletariat. This consisted, with the coming into being of towns, of the group of artisans who were unable to enter the guilds. Their equivalent in the country was the prosperous peasant, and during this period the rise in the wool trade enabled many farming families to be manufacturers and even traders, and thus to become at least partly independent of the business of agricultural produce.

The middle class consisted both of officials, such as the reeve or sheriff, and of tradesmen, such as millers, about whose way of life we learn a lot from Chaucer. They might own property or rent it, but were characterized chiefly by something they lacked: they did not aspire to wear a coat of arms. One should not underestimate the power and importance of these people, when they acted as a group. The burgesses – townsmen with certain traditional and legal rights within their towns – had long been an important element in English politics and social history. On the Continent their equivalents, the burghers, were sometimes, even at this date, more powerful than kings. The Flemish burghers, for instance, made independent decisions in defiance of their ruler, the Count of Flanders, by siding with the English during the Hundred Years War, leaving him powerless as a nominal supporter of the king of France. It was these same people, flexing new economic muscles, who boosted the prosperity of the wool trade through East Anglia, making that region an important centre of the English economy at this time. Contact with them, and the freedom given by the trade itself, had two effects. It gave to a new element in English life an awareness of its own power; and it set in motion a new commercial and trading culture, with standards altogether different from the medieval set of knightly values.

Meanwhile the knightly class was itself in a state of change. It retained, not without some sense of rearguard action, its traditional prerogatives: restricted heraldry, forming a national link of relationships; French culture and customs; patronage of the arts. Through the rural system of administration these old shire families controlled local opinion and supervised local life in much of the country. But at court, and at the centre of political activity, a new power structure was emerging. The great magnates and their vast households were of a different class. They (themselves largely descendants of wealthy knights and minor barons) were powerful on a national, not a local, scale. They belonged to no specific part of the country, having widely scattered possessions, which theoretically they held in feudal tenure from the Crown. While the knights, and at first most of the magnates, would be largely French-speaking, English was gaining momentum at the court itself, and elsewhere through the medium of the law. The literature of the time shows us, however, that all powerful people would have been completely bilingual.

It is to this class, the great magnates, that England's subsequent great families belonged. Many of their names now strike us as familiar: the Beauchamps, the Earls of Warwick, the Mortimers, the Mowbrays, the Staffords and the Courtenays. More regional, and to begin with less central also in power, were the rising families of the Percys and the Nevilles, loyal Lancastrians with territories stretching from Yorkshire to the Border. We have to think of them all as being immensely rich, their wealth derived from gifts of land and grants of office from the Crown, and distributed through their households and retainers and paid supporters. It is estimated that in present-day values the annual income of a knight or an ordinary peer would be between £3,000 and £6,000 and that of a magnate between £60,000 and £90,000. Though he was an exceptional case, being the uncle of the king and the most powerful citizen in Britain, John of Gaunt when he died had an income from property of some £390,000 per annum in today's terms.

Some sort of feeling of unity was supplied by the national,

rather than regional, interests of these men; and the local knightly families gave a cultural unity throughout the land. But on the whole the England of our period was remarkably diverse, with local variations of life-style and of language. Shire rivalries maintained the permanent possibility of division within the kingdom. Roads – many based on the great Roman thoroughfares, and many of course still in use today – ran the length of the land, but we learn from Langland that they were considered most unsafe. Bandits and outlawed 'foresters' ganged up, sometimes in large numbers, and forced ransoms out of prosperous travellers. The largely wild nature of the country off the highway enabled them to live their unurbanized life more or less unmolested. The mid-fourteenth century is the age of Robin Hood, whose story developed in popular ballad form at this time.

Into this slowly developing England came an outside influence which was to shake and change the evolution of our land, and to bedevil the spirit of Richard's reign as persistently as Mount Vesuvius or the nuclear bomb have haunted the subconscious of other ages.

Bubonic plague is caused by the bacillus *Pasteurella pestis*, carried by rats and spread among them, and from them to humans, by the rat flea. The bacilli multiply in the blood of the rat and, being drawn into the feeding flea, begin to obstruct its stomach. When the rat dies the flea, now hungry because of the difficulty of sucking blood, seeks other sources of food, usually human. In an attempt to draw in blood from humans it releases infected blood from its stomach which then enters the bite wound and infects the host. At the same time the blood from crushed fleas may enter scratches or wounds, and the process accelerates. The name of this form of plague derives from its chief symptom, the bubo, a glandular swelling in the groin, the armpit, or the neck. Black and blue marks about the body then result from subcutaneous haemorrhages. Fever sets in within a few days of infection, increasing rapidly until the patient collapses in a coma, and normally within five days death results through heart failure or internal bleeding. Some may recover, but the mortality rate is between sixty and eighty-five per cent.

The plague had existed in Europe since Roman times, destroying about half the population of the Empire in the mid-

A German *Pestblätte*, a sort of amulet carried for protection against the Black Death.

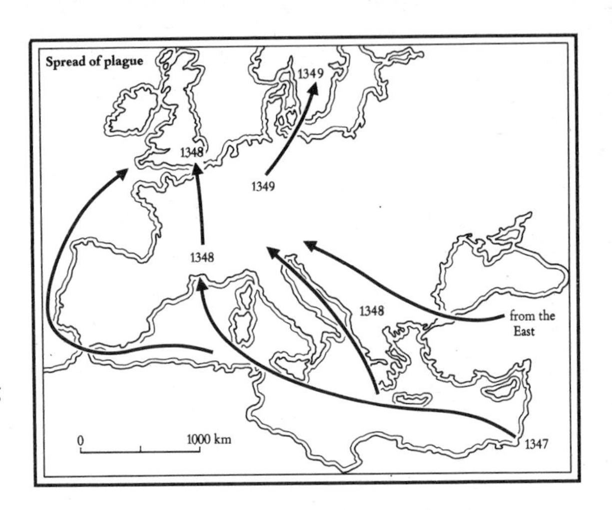

RIGHT A map to show the spread of the bubonic plague from China into Europe in the fourteenth century.

BELOW St Roch, the patron saint of plague sufferers, shows a tell-tale contusion on his leg; the skin discoloration resulting from haemorrhaging under the skin was the mark of the 'Black' Death.

ABOVE The mass deaths of the terrible pandemic which swept through Europe in the fourteenth century are graphically depicted in this scene from a contemporary French manuscript.

RIGHT The sudden reduction in the rural population caused by the Black Death led to a change in the settlement pattern. The field marks in this aerial view of Tusmore in Oxfordshire show the outline of a village deserted at this time and never reoccupied.

sixth century. The great outbreak, or pandemic, of the fourteenth century, called the Black Death from the symptom of skin discoloration, killed some 25,000,000 of the population of Europe, reaching England in the year 1348. It lasted then for about a year, but returned in the 1360s and in all reduced the population by about half. Exact figures are difficult to determine. Contemporary records are likely to be exaggerated, but the result was undeniably the sudden reversal of a previously steady growth of a settled population.

The effects of this trauma on the social and the economic structure had political results which crucially affected the patch of history through which Richard lived; and the psychological effects must have been every bit as shattering, particularly since the sufferers had to live with the insecurity of ignorance of the disaster's causes. Astrological and theological explanations were advanced, but they must have left the puzzle as to why God should be so terrifyingly angry or the stars so arbitrarily unfair. Combined with the rising spirit of economic awareness and independence of mind, this shake-up of a steadily evolving nation set in motion processes with which, at the very start of his reign, Richard found himself obliged to deal.

For all these reasons the world in which Richard became king was very different from the heroic and adventurous world of his father and grandfather into which he had been born.

> Sir Richard de Pontchardon, who was then the Marshal of Aquitaine, came in at that moment and said to me: 'Froissart, write down and record that her Highness the Princess has given birth to a fine boy.'

He came into the world on a Wednesday, at the stroke of ten.

It was Epiphany, the January of 1367. Jean Froissart, the assiduous chronicler of life in England and France during our period, was 'in Bordeaux, sitting at table', at the court of the Black Prince, Edward of Woodstock, Prince of Wales, when the future king of England was born: 'He came into the world on a Wednesday, at the stroke of ten.' The fact that they were at Bordeaux at all was the culmination of a long sequence of events in Anglo-French history – the tumultuous political background to the monarchy which Richard was to inherit, and which in its turn had a critical effect on the progress of his reign.

Anybody familiar with the over-simplifications of history

will not be surprised to learn that the Hundred Years War did not last a hundred years. In fact it spread rather loosely over a longer span, from the late 1330s to the early 1450s; it was not, either, anything which could continuously be recognized as a war, since there were several long periods of truce and much desultory skirmishing, the actual spells of warfare being comparatively short and isolated. But during this very long period France and England enjoyed no settled peace.

War between the two countries started in the time of Richard's grandfather, Edward III, who succeeded to the throne at an early age and quickly showed a confidence and ability much more akin to the temperament of his own grandfather, Edward I, than to the weak and foolish character of his father, Edward II. He was, by all accounts, a splendid man, and the glory of his personality and achievements must still have glowed in Richard, to flare out on those few but important occasions when we shall see him undertaking spontaneous acts of personal courage.

England at the time controlled Gascony, the valuable wine-growing area of France at the south of the Plantagenet fiefdom of Aquitaine, bordering the Bay of Biscay. To the north of France the wool trade with Flanders formed a bond between the Flemish and the English which might at any time become uncomfortable for the French. Edward increased their discomfort by marrying the daughter of the Count of Hainault, a territory at the south of the Low Countries on the French border, and important strategically in terms of French freedom for expansion. These circumstances led to a state of tension between the two countries, which the French further increased by lending their support to the Scots when they began to make disconcerting attacks on England.

These were not the overt reasons for the start of the Hundred Years War, but they were probably the real ones. The overt reasons concern the inter-relationship of the royal houses of England and France and the resulting problems of succession. Charles IV, known as Charles le Bel, who died without an heir, was uncle to the young Edward III; and Philippe de Valois, who succeeded Charles, was Edward's distant cousin. The English argued that Edward's mother, Isabella, who was yet to live another thirty years, had a better claim to the French throne,

ABOVE The marriage of Edward III and Philippa of Hainault.

RIGHT Edward III: an illustration from a fifteenth-century manuscript.

Aftir him regned his son ful right
The prudde Edward þat doughti knight.
vij sonys he hadd truli here.
That to him were bothe lefe & dere.
First þe king did a grete maistrey.
Atte Scluce he wanned a grete scabe.
Atte Cresse he ffaught þere agayn.
The king of Beme þer was sleine.
And þe king of ffraunce put to flight.
No lenger þan durst he fight.

A Sege at Calice he lei bifore.
That lestid twelve mounthe and more.
And er he thens wuld go.
He wanne Calice and townis mo.
At the bataille of Peitowe bi ordenaunce.
Was take þon the king off ffraunce.
At Westmenstre he lieth þere.
He regned alle most l yere.
Aftir him deid prince Edward
Whiche had a son that hete Richard.

An assembly of French nobles discuss the complex question of the succession to the French throne after the death of Charles IV.

but since the French argued convincingly against the crown passing to a woman, Edward himself then claimed a 'closer degree of kinship' to his uncle Charles than that possessed by de Valois, who was only Charles's cousin.

The French had made their choice – Philippe had been appointed king by the assembly of peers – and Edward's claim can hardly have been seriously maintained. It was undoubtedly of more significance that, by a victory in Flanders, the new French king had interfered with the smooth progress of the Flemish wool trade. But we shall find throughout this story that mere political or economic aims had always to be supported by a claim of justice and legitimacy. That was part of the knightly code of conduct, and it still regulated the acts of kings and nobles in the time of Richard II.

At the same time the Plantagenet fief of Aquitaine was under threat of seizure by the French, who were also still abetting the attacks made by the Scots. Hostilities erupted in 1337, and after several inconclusive expeditions the English launched a major attack on Normandy in 1344.

The most striking thing about the campaign in Normandy is its lack of relevance to any of the causes of the war. Edward was in theory on his way to Gascony, where his garrisons were being besieged, but the wind was against them, and they had heard that Normandy was rich. This chance occurrence is of double significance: it set up expectations for the war which were later to turn sour on England; and because it led to the victory of Crécy it established English presence on French soil to the extent of ensuring that the war would continue. The first of these effects was to have repercussions in the reign of Richard. The booty shipped from Normandy, and the valuable ransoms obtained, more than paid for the expenses of the war; Edward, we are told, was able to pay his soldiers well. But when the Hundred Years War stopped being profitable and started being a national expense, the king was in trouble.

Crécy was the first campaign, and the first success, of the Black Prince, Richard's father. Edward had put him in charge of the forward division, intending that this battle should be his. The king and his own division stayed in the background throughout, and at one point, according to Froissart, he even refused to go to his son's aid when his party was being hard

The Battle of Crécy, 1346, at which Edward finally defeated the French.

pressed: 'Go back to him and the people who have sent you, and tell them not to send for me again today, while my son is still alive. My orders are that the boy should win his spurs, and if God wills it I wish this day and the honour of it to be his.'

The boy was only sixteen. We are constantly coming up against the shock of the youth of these heroes, and the terrible brevity of some of their lives. From the success of Crécy his fortunes went forward, as his father had generously intended, until as commander-in-chief, without his father's help, he won the crucial battle of Poitiers at the age of twenty-five. The king of France was captured amid devastating losses, and English domination of the territory around Bordeaux was for the time being secured. 'In war and in love', says Froissart, 'it happens frequently that fortune is more wonderfully kind than one would dare to hope.' The Prince of Wales rode back to Bordeaux as its virtual ruler, taking with him the captured king.

That was in 1356, and it is significant that we find him there some twelve years later, when his son was born. Much had of course intervened, the war continuing. Peace terms had been agreed at Brétigny, near Chartres, in October 1360. England was to keep Aquitaine, Calais, and the area of the Somme. In return for free possession of these lands, Edward renounced his claim to the French throne. The captured French king was to pay a vast ransom, a further boost to the popular idea of the war's profitability, and so probably a contribution to the misleading trend which was eventually to undermine the British economy. In the event most of these terms were broken, and only a portion of the ransom paid. But at the time it must have seemed a notable English success.

The Black Prince returned to France in 1363 as 'Prince of Aquitaine', sent to govern what was now virtually a new English province. (His nickname, we are told, was due to the

Soldiers looting a conquered city during the Hundred Years War. In the early phases of the war the booty and ransoms more than paid for the expenses of the campaigns.

uant le roy sceut
ces nouuelles ⁊
la certainete du
dist au
gaultie
ioyes d

The English siege of Calais ends in a victorious assault, seen here in an illustration from an early copy of Froissart's *Chronicles*.

RIGHT A medieval knight. The knights were an immensely powerful and influential group within the court.

BELOW A typical fourteenth-century scene of jousting, an occupation much favoured by the Black Prince, who ran an extravagant and sizeable court, with a pronounced military flavour.

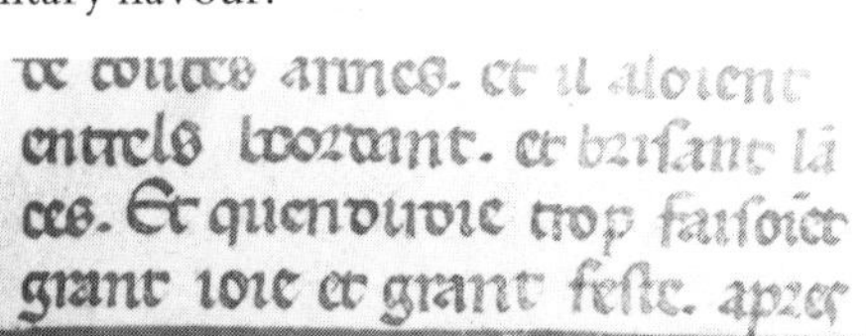

'black' terror he inspired by the fierceness of his fighting. It was probably a later invention, however, and at the time he was known as Prince of Wales.) Signs now began to appear of his fatal extravagance, a weakness which was to increase and indeed be inherited by his son. We know that he maintained at Bordeaux a large and expensive court. Unlike the court of his father and Queen Philippa, a luxurious environment in which Geoffrey Chaucer was present at the time of Richard's birth, the Black Prince's court was military, proving a constant state of readiness for war. Richard himself was to change the style again, preferring a more formal and refined way of life than his father and grandfather had chosen. One modifying factor in the style of court life into which Richard was born must, however, have been the gentle character of the Princess of Wales, Joan of Kent, who was then aged twenty-nine.

Edward of Woodstock, Prince of Wales, had married, in 1361, his cousin Joan, the 'Fair Maid of Kent' and widow of Sir Thomas Holland. Her initial marriage, to the Earl of Salisbury, had for political reasons been set aside. Froissart tells us that Bolingbroke later implied that she had been unfaithful to the Black Prince at Bordeaux, and that Richard's striking differences in character from his father were due to his actually being the son of some 'young and handsome' attendant at his court. But what little Froissart tells us of the Princess rather indicates a loyal and constant companion, and at least we have no doubt of Richard's subsequent devotion to his mother. At the time of the crisis of the Peasants' Revolt, at the height of the country's turmoil and at the peak of his own danger, he spent a night comforting her after the fear and humiliation she had suffered.

But that is still far in the future. From the glorious victory of Poitiers a long military decline was to lead to the disappointment of the royal hopes of England, and a state of affairs which was far from satisfactory at the start of the new reign.

2
The Start of a Reign

RICHARD HAD an elder brother, Edward, whose natural destiny as king of England was denied by his early death in 1371. Richard's father, in the meantime, schooled and trained from boyhood to be heir to the throne, continued his virtual reign at Bordeaux as Edward III entered his sixties. His grasp of policy had never been strong, and his enthusiastic militancy continued undiminished while the situation around him began to crumble. After Richard's birth he undertook a misjudged expedition to Castile, which proved costly, while the loot and forfeiture of war had ceased to flow. The direct result was a set of taxes imposed on Gascony which succeeded in alienating the Gascon lords from England. Richard was, as we shall see, unfortunately too young to learn from this mistake.

War was renewed, and the Black Prince went on his last campaign. Battle was his lifelong hobby, and no doubt the relative length of the peace had troubled him. He was, it is clear, a straightforward, spontaneous man, with a simple love of his colourful life. He had started early and worked hard, and now, at the age of forty, he found himself declining. When he went to the siege of Limoges he was no longer able to ride, and had to be carried on a litter, suffering, it appears, from dropsy. The siege was successful, Limoges taken, but from then on other cities began to side with the French. And Prince Edward, broken in spirit as much as in health, retired to England in 1371.

He died at the Palace of Westminster in June 1376, the year of his father's jubilee. It is rare for an English monarch to occupy the throne for a full fifty years (but of course Edward had started his reign at the age of fifteen), and at Christmas that year the ageing king proclaimed Richard his heir, parading the child before the nobles and officials of the city. Then he fell ill, and for several months the affairs of the nation were dealt with by his son, John of Gaunt, Duke of Lancaster.

When Edward died on 21 June 1377, he had three surviving sons, and Richard, his grandson, was a boy of ten. Experience throughout Europe told of the perils of a royal minority, and it cannot have seemed wise to follow Edward's directions and crown Richard. Nevertheless there seems to have been consensus that Richard was the rightful heir, and some feeling of urgency that this should be officially established. The French had maintained a fleet in the Channel during Edward's illness,

PREVIOUS PAGE Richard II, presiding over his court, is presented with a book.

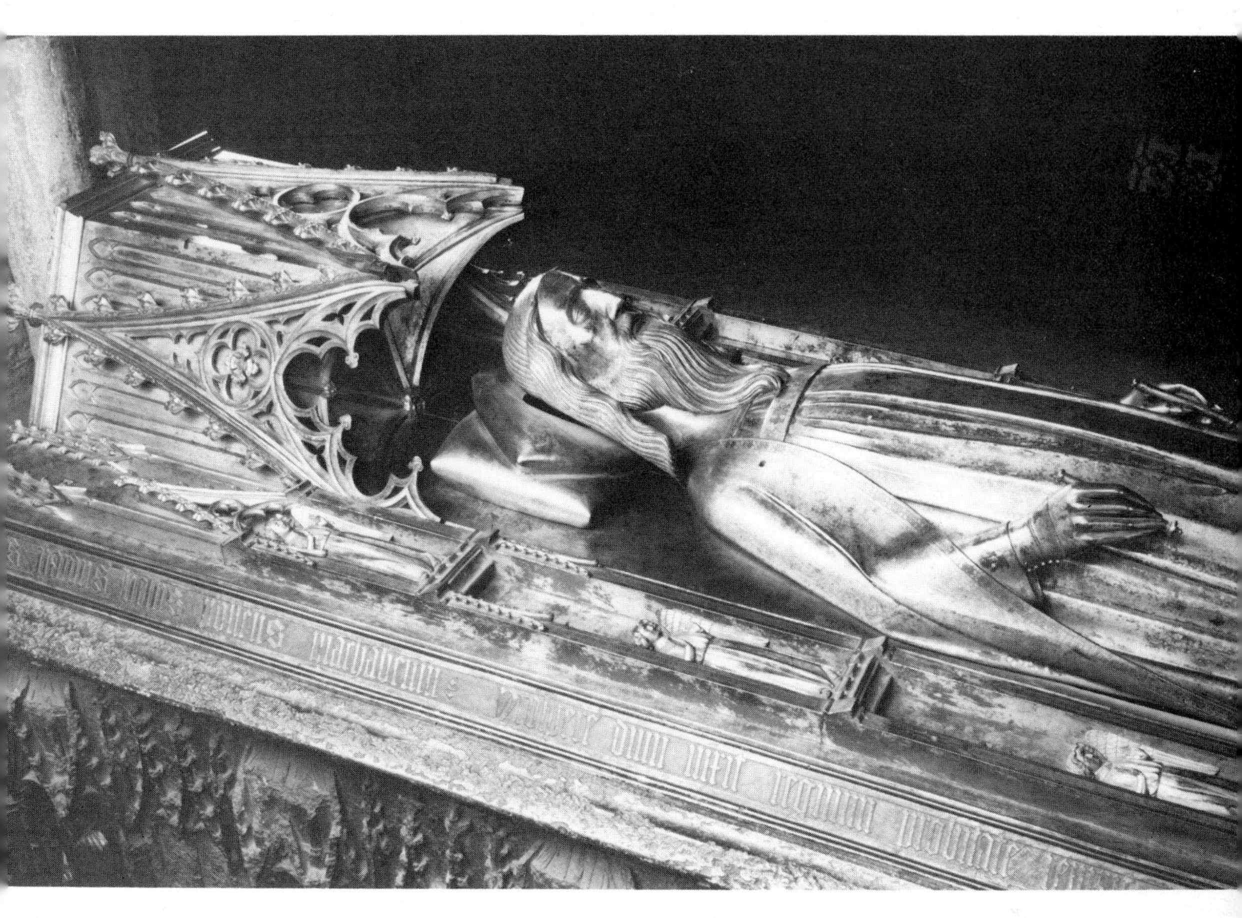

The gilt-bronze effigy of Edward III lies at the side of the shrine of Edward the Confessor in Westminster Abbey, not far from the tomb of his grandson Richard.

and a week after his death they landed on the south coast. No doubt neither side had forgotten the circumstances under which Edward himself had landed in France as claimant to the throne, and the disastrous long-term results. Richard was crowned in July, and at once his uncles left for the south to oust the French.

Richard's coronation appears, nevertheless, to have been a suitably sumptuous affair. Processions took place the previous day, and the fountains of London ran with wine. Richard was crowned by the Archbishop of Canterbury, Simon Sudbury, whose loyalty was later to be repaid by death at the hands of rebellious peasants. John of Gaunt presided in several capacities over some of the rituals. The chronicler Walsingham tells us that the ceremonials included a state banquet following the long religious service, and the whole event evidently proved a long, hard day. The child king was so exhausted at the end that he had to be carried back to his palace on the shoulders of his tutor and

friend, Sir Simon Burley, and the report touchingly mentions that he lost one of his slippers in the process. Six centuries later we can see him now in his royal regalia, on a panel in Westminster Abbey, where the event took place. Serious and upright, with a brave attempt at dignity, he sits perched on his throne, encumbered by regalia. It has been credibly suggested that the effect of such an awe-inspiring ceremony on a child of ten may account for Richard's lifelong and exaggerated awareness of the importance of being a king.

He was seventh in the line of undisputed monarchs descended from Henry II, a dynasty of England unrivalled in its span and in its European power. They took the name Plantagenet from a habit of their ancestor, Geoffrey, Count of Anjou, who wore in his hat a sprig of broom, in Latin *planta genista, genêt* in French, adopted as a gesture of humility during a pilgrimage to the Holy Land, and later used as the Angevin family crest. Henry I of England inherited from his father William the Conqueror both the crown of England and the dukedom of Normandy, and married his daughter Matilda to his greatest continental rival, Geoffrey of Anjou. Since no male heir survived, Matilda's son Henry in due course inherited these combined titles, and by marriage to the daughter and heiress of the Duke of Aquitaine became the ruler not only of England, but of much of France. He was succeeded by his two sons Richard and John, from whom the English monarchy passed in direct succession by the eldest son through four generations to Richard II's grandfather, Edward. The rivalry with France was an inevitable result of the former possession of this power, and the decline of England's grip on its foreign territories reached its critical phase at the start of Richard's reign.

If the hurried departure from the coronation was a symptom of the threat to Richard's kingdom from elsewhere, there were very soon signs of the dangerous cracking of the structure from within. The king himself was, for a considerable time, by no means the most powerful person in the realm. It is significant in view of later events that one of his acts at his coronation was to create for Henry Percy the new earldom of Northumberland. There, sufficiently far removed from London, the Percys ruled over what was virtually an independent kingdom. Clearly the act of ennoblement which appeared to recognize this

OPPOSITE The tomb of the Black Prince, Richard's father, in Canterbury Cathedral.

importance was not the decision of the child king, and the granting of titles (and with them the wealth of territory) to his uncle Thomas, already Duke of Gloucester and now Earl of Kent, probably signified the power and acquisitiveness of the family surrounding him. But certainly the most influential and by far the richest of his relatives was his uncle John, Duke of Lancaster.

John of Gaunt was so called from his birthplace of Ghent. He was the fourth son of Edward III, aged thirty-seven at Richard's accession, and already highly experienced in government and international diplomacy. Essentially he seems to have been a politician, rather than a soldier, and his influence over English affairs had already become extremely powerful during the joint illnesses of the king and the Prince of Wales. He had acquired his titles and his wealth partly by dextrous marriages: firstly to Blanche, the heiress of the house of Lancaster, from which marriage he obtained the dukedom, the official title being bestowed on him by his father when he was twenty-two; and secondly, two years after Blanche's death in the autumn of 1369, to Constance, daughter of King Pedro of Castile, thus inheriting a claim to the Castilian crown which, however, was to prove difficult to establish. For much of his married life he neglected poor Constance, and lived with his mistress Katherine Swynford.

As a child John had been created Earl of Richmond, and the king later made him Earl of Lincoln, of Leicester, and of Derby. He used his vast wealth to support a considerable household, distinguishing his retinue by the use of a collar with the sign SS, a mark which may have seemed to imply a court to rival the king's. Certainly he had the power and wealth to run his own private army, and indeed promoted his affairs with his own knights in independence of national policy. He had a palace on the Thames, the Savoy, so called because it had been built in the previous century by Peter of Savoy, from whom it passed through his niece, the queen of Henry III, to the Duchy of

An illustration from Froissart's *Chronicles*, showing Richard II and the Duke of Gloucester, his uncle.

Lancaster. The site is occupied now by the Savoy Chapel, the Savoy Theatre, and the famous hotel. Geoffrey Chaucer's wife, Philippa, was a servant to the Duchess, and Chaucer himself received from Gaunt an annual allowance and several minor offices.

Inevitably this royal uncle had considerable influence at the start of the boy Richard's reign. His relations with Richard were sometimes tense, and had their stormy moments, but reconciliations provided at least a nominal friendliness over the years. Although he does not seem to have had aspirations to the throne, there was from the start the undecided question of the succession hanging over Gaunt's position. Richard had succeeded as the son of the eldest son. The next in line to the Black Prince, Lionel, Duke of Clarence, had also died before his father, leaving a daughter, Philippa. Edmund Mortimer, Earl of March, had married this heiress, and the fact that at the king's funeral he had walked behind the coffin with Edward's three surviving sons is a clear indication of the status of his relationship. We have seen several times already that in this period a title might be inherited by marriage to the heiress.

In Richard's first years as king, Gaunt more or less ruled with the tacit rivalry of the Earl of March. The power of the Duke, however, asserted itself quickly, and the Earl providently accepted a post as Royal Lieutenant to Ireland in 1378. He was to die there three years later as the result of an attack of pneumonia caught while crossing a river in County Cork. However, his death was not the end of this particular rivalry, since from these two were descended the houses of Lancaster and York which were to tear England apart with warfare for most of the century after Richard's death. The ambiguity of possible succession through the female line and thus via March, as against the male line of the House of Lancaster, remained a problem, and it was March's descendant who ended the Lancastrian dynasty's reign by becoming king as Edward IV. But for the time being Gaunt had the field to himself.

He was, it seems, as unpopular as he was rich, and much of the bad feeling which dogged Richard's reign can be laid at his door, arising through no fault of the king's during these years of his minority. Long before the Peasants' Revolt, Gaunt found himself having to flee the London mob. When that unnerving uprising eventually broke out Gaunt showed that his diplomacy included the wisdom of caution, and did the safest thing he could. He kept as far away from it as possible.

Richard remained under the control of Gaunt and the council of magnates until he was nearly twenty-two, an unusually long minority for a king to suffer, and a symptom both of his diffidence and of their power. There were others at court who checked to some extent the Duke's will, such as the new Earl of Northumberland, Henry Percy. No official regency was announced, and Richard was throughout the period nominally a reigning king. Much of the focus of government centred on the London home of the king's mother, John of Gaunt's sister-in-law, Princess Joan, Princess of Wales. Froissart speaks of her with evident approval, and the long knowledge she had of the Bordeaux court, the Gascon occupation and the French wars must have given her the stability of experience during the troubled years which followed.

Although the formidable influence of his superiors in age and experience prevented him at first from exercising political

The Privy Seal of John of Gaunt.

John of Gaunt, one of whose daughters married into the Portuguese royal house, is seen here at a feast given by King John I of Portugal. He is seated to the right of the king. The picture shows the exaggerated styles of dress which were also fashionable at Richard's court, the points of the shoes having become so long that, as the figure on the right demonstrates, they presented problems in walking.

power, Richard seems to have imposed his personal tastes and style on his court from an early stage. He encouraged a refinement and formality which his father's more military circumstances clearly lacked. He possessed a library of fine illuminated manuscripts in both French and English, some of which he acquired in his early youth. We shall see later how these literary tastes affected the course of English literature. He loved adornment (his personal jewellery was elaborate and artistic), dressed in a sophisticated and modish way, and was evidently sufficiently vain to commission an unusual number of portraits of himself.

One symptom of the isolation of Richard's youth, and a partial cause of the alienation from his elders which gave rise to trouble in the central period of his reign, was his acquisition of intimate companions of around his own age. Romantic friendships between men were a fashionable affectation; there is no suggestion, though, that Richard may have indulged in a more physical form of relationship, and the memory of the scandalous conduct of his great-grandfather Edward II was still a historical embarrassment. Richard's two main friends were respectable and apparently sound, and for a time he avoided the jealousies and internal courtly tensions of undue favouritism. That this was a constant danger became apparent later, when his uncles began to resent the excessive power and influence bestowed on Robert de Vere.

De Vere was already an aristocrat, being the ninth Earl of Oxford, and he was five years older than Richard. Later he married the king's cousin, and after Richard's marriage he continued to be a part of the central court. Another close friend appears to have been Thomas Mowbray, who, like de Vere, had private apartments in the royal palace. Mowbray was a year older than Richard, a member of an old baronial family, though he later became Earl of Nottingham and eventually Duke of Norfolk. The close initial relations between the king and these

A typical scene of jousting outside a castle of the period, the ladies as usual watching from the battlements, and much detailed medieval activity taking place all around. Here again we see the refinement of the fashionable costume, the tight hose and belted tunic.

associates could not be sustained, and Mowbray in the end died in Venice, in exile. But we shall be hearing more of both these men in later phases of Richard's troubled story.

At the beginning of Richard's reign the war with France was continuing, and French success led increasingly to its being a drain on English finances. Instead of producing booty and ransoms, it now had to be paid for. This was plainly no fault of Richard's, though he was to find himself enmeshed in the results. He seems instinctively always to have favoured peaceful solutions, and his later second marriage, to a French princess, was perhaps the nearest the two countries came to a permanent alliance during this period. It is perhaps typical that he hesitated, even when pressed, to go on a crusade. And although his expeditions to Ireland have the look of militancy, in fact, as we shall see, his policy was conciliation and collaboration. It was ironic that a futile French war which he would have wished to stop should undermine his economy, with permanent effects.

To begin with, the costs of war had been borne by taxes on the gentry and the burgesses, who, it might be supposed, could best afford to pay them. In 1379, however, Parliament authorized a poll tax, a tax, that is, which covered every person; though the tax that year was graduated so that the burden fell less severely on those who had less to spare, and the rich were encouraged to take care of the poor. The aim was to spread the load of the exorbitant costs of war, and relieve the minority of some of the financial burden. Handled with care, this might have succeeded. But the Parliament of 1380 made a radical and inexplicable mistake. It instituted a level tax, and at the same time increased the rate from one groat (fourpence) to three groats (one shilling) a head. A shilling a head was a significant amount, worth perhaps £1.50 in present-day values, and we have to remember that under the ancient agricultural system still persisting in many parts of the country many peasant farmers possessed no cash income at all. So great were the differences at that time between the rich and the poor that a level poll tax made no sense at all, and one wonders how parliament could have seriously expected to impose it.

The causes of the Peasants' Revolt are many and fascinating, and it would be neither fair nor honest to over-simplify them.

There is no doubt that at the root of the trouble lay the Black Death, the memory of it and its multiple effects on English society and the economic structure of the country. The plague had returned briefly in 1379, and no doubt this reminder served as an awful warning. Life was short and perilous. Everybody, in the end, was on his own, and must protect his own interests. This certainly seems to have been the growing spirit of the second half of the century.

Nothing new came suddenly into being with the institution of the poll tax of 1381. The uprising which followed was part of a continuing process, more a symptom than a cause of change: from about 1370 the peasants had been forming confederacies and refusing service. Part of the cause of the Peasants' Revolt of 1381 was their new awareness of power, and their expectations of prosperity.

One of the clearest effects of the Black Death had been the sudden reduction of the rural workforce. This more than anything undermined the previously stable system, the lord-villein relationship, the manor and the holding. Holdings fell vacant, and new occupants brought an awareness of the possibility of mobility. Landlords attempted less labour-intensive farming, such as stock rearing, but in spite of all this the emergence of a new factor in the economy could not be ignored: labour had become a marketable commodity.

Much that then happened has a remarkably familiar ring to it. The Government attempted to impose artificial controls. The Statute of Labourers of 1351 aimed to hold down both wages and prices; but the market has an inevitable tendency to reassert itself, and there was both resentment and evasion. Laws were passed to prevent the mobility of the labour force, but at the same time the villeins combined into leagues to refuse their traditional service. In an agricultural situation, where labour demands are imposed by conditions and seasons rather than by plan, what could be done? As the cost of hired labour went up the landlords conspired with the labourers by illegally paying what they demanded. Farm profits too were increasing, and no doubt the market forces settled, as they tend to, for a state which, unlike the preceding centuries of exploitation, was no more than realistic. Several major changes in the social structure quickly followed.

Life begins to improve: timber was a main source of fuel and building material (ABOVE) and food more plentiful. Bees were kept for honey (BELOW LEFT) and peasants took their corn to the windmill to be ground (BELOW RIGHT).

Firstly there came into existence a new class, and with it a new attitude. The roving labourers – villeins who had abandoned their holdings, an itinerant force which was able (particularly at harvest time) to establish its own values – gave both to themselves and to their landbound contemporaries a sense of power and choice. At the same time, from the 1370s onwards, the increasing tendency on the part of landowners to lease their land rather than farm it personally had produced a tenant body which, prospering by the wool trade, gave rise to a new idea of yeoman independence. All these factors, occurring simultaneously, increased resistance to demands for servitude. We find a marked improvement in peasant diet taking place during the 1370s and 80s, a further result of their economic power after the population decline, and a further spur to expectation and to the realization of what life could have been like all the time.

A rural proletariat and the making of a yeoman class: with these innovations came a marked sense of class consciousness which had not previously been possible in the rural areas. There was scepticism about the naturalness of the current distribution of power and resources, and about the injustice of the burden of labour. A popular ballad of the time (sometimes attributed to the ecclesiastical agitator John Ball, one of the leaders of the revolt) sums this up:

> When Adam delved and Eve span,
> Who was then the gentleman?

We have already remarked that magnates such as John of Gaunt were liable to attack, during Richard's minority, by the London mob. Such unrest and aggression was now a spirit which was spreading to the country.

Froissart attributes the cause of the revolt to the rising prosperity of the peasantry, and as a simple analysis this seems accurate enough. He points out that a greater degree of serfdom survived in England than in other countries, and that it was most prevalent in the counties of Kent and Essex where the trouble broke out – though in the case of Kent the truth of this is doubtful. People said that when the world began there were no serfs. Men were no longer willing to be treated as animals; they had a consciousness of their own humanity. 'If they worked for

Adam hic vestitus e(st) ad laborandum & Eva sedet & lactet filiu(m) suu(m) Abel & stat iuxta eam quasi puer

Filii Adam · Cayn · Abel · Seth ·

Et factum est omne tempus Seth dcccc xii

Factu(m) est omne tempus quo vixit Adam · dcccc xxx ·

avertis inimicis

LEFT A contemporary sketch illustrates the popular verse:

When Adam delved and Eve span,
Who was then the gentleman?

The egalitarian arguments of John Ball used the reasoning that men were originally equal.

The flourishing of the wool trade at this time gave rise to a new prosperity among the rural and the burgess classes. ABOVE A lady weaving. BELOW Cloth is dyed in a heated vat.

their lords, they wanted to have wages for doing so.' John Ball, several times imprisoned by the Archbishop of Canterbury for stirring up the rabble, but rashly released each time to continue doing so, had the habit of preaching egalitarianism to the people coming from church on Sundays. As a priest without a benefice he had a grudge against the clergy, but his main theme was insurrection in the cause of equality: 'Goods should be held in common. There should be no more segregation into the classes of gentlemen and villeins. Why are some people more powerful than others? Have they earned that right? We are all descended equally from Adam and Eve: why then should some hold others in subjection? They wear ermine, we wear rags; they drink wine, we drink water. They are comfortable in their big houses, while we are out in the fields. It is our sweat which keeps them in luxury.' John Ball was not the last to say such things, but the immediate result was that his programme was proved unrealistic. The Archbishop sent him back to prison.

They wear ermine, we wear rags; they drink wine, we drink water.

One of the things he suggested, Froissart says, was a petition to the king. He is young, Ball argued, and if confronted by sufficient determination he would put right our wrongs, either because he would sympathize or because he would see that there was no alternative. 'If we went in earnest and together, many serfs and subjected people would follow to win freedom.' The ideas he put forward in Kent spread to the capital, and met encouragement from the restive London mob. No doubt the trail of pilgrims to the shrine of St Thomas at Canterbury provided a two-way flow of opinion, and the people of Kent received support in their intention to march on the capital.

What actually happened was not, of course, the result of the ideas put forward by one man. A pre-existing spirit of revolt was sparked into conflagration by a series of fairly clear-cut events. There had been enormous evasion of the 1380 poll tax. As many as a third of the people who had paid in 1379 avoided paying. The shortfall was so clear that it demanded action. In Suffolk alone some 27,000 were, by the first count, apparently missing. An immediate revision put some of this right, but still some 14,000 remained to be accounted for. The population of the greater part of England appeared to have dropped by about 45,000 between 1377 and 1381. If the poll tax had been intended as a radical solution to the need for revenue, it had failed.

Significantly the rebels did not blame Richard himself for the tax. Their slogan, when they eventually marched, was one of allegiance to 'Kynge Richard and the trew communes'. The 'traitors' they set out to punish were the king's ministers, particularly the Chancellor, who was also that same Archbishop who had imprisoned Ball, and the Treasurer. Their quarrel was with them on the one hand, and with their local lords on the other. It is probable that when they called these people 'traitors' they thought of them as traitors to the king as well as to the nation. Froissart is probably right when he says they were going to London to draw the King's attention to the situation.

If this is so, then Richard's minority was itself a contributory factor to the Peasants' Revolt. We might speculate that had he been of age he would not have allowed it to happen. Certainly when at a later point in his career he made a similar mistake, which was to be a major cause of his downfall, he appeared to have learned at least a partial lesson from this earlier disaster. The problem on both occasions was financial: Richard or his central Government had to raise money, and urgently, from somewhere in order to maintain the security of his position. The moral, no doubt, is that one should live within one's means. But Richard's was not the temperament of a man capable of doing so.

3 The Peasants' Revolt

Ichã balle

THE RESPONSE to the embarrassing shortfall in the collection of the poll tax was the immediate appointment of commissions of inquiry. These began to sit in January 1381, and by the threat of arrest they succeeded in increasing the returns. On 1 June an inquiry commission session at Brentwood in Essex gave rise to angry exchanges and threats, which resulted in the villagers combining with those of neighbouring fishing villages to present a front against the lawyers, who were duly intimidated. This situation was taken seriously by the Government, and the Chief Justice of Common Pleas was sent to Essex to hear indictments. Defensive opposition was intensified by this move. The lawyers, as agents of the Government's will, had become identified with the hated tax, and it was against them that much of the energy of the rising was directed.

Resistance spread within Essex, and help was sought and given from Kent. Open revolt broke out at Gravesend after the arrest of an escaped villein, who was imprisoned in Rochester Castle. The insurgents took the castle and set free the prisoners. At Maidstone in Kent there was a bout of looting, and John Ball, the provocative priest, was freed from Maidstone jail, where Archbishop Sudbury had confined him. The people of Maidstone appointed a captain, who thus became the leader of the revolt.

Not much is known about Wat Tyler, except from his actions. He was indeed, Froissart tells us, a tiler. Froissart disliked him intensely. It seems likely that he had served as a soldier in France, and certainly much of the form of the rising shows military experience. Many English villagers must inevitably have had some practice in warfare, and the very fact of electing a captain shows a sense of discipline and planning which is not typical of an angry mob. Right from the start we get a sense that they were determined and clear about their intentions.

Tyler's second-in-command seems to have been a man called Jack Straw, about whom also little is known, with John Ball acting as adviser. In East Anglia the spreading revolt produced as leader a man called Geoffrey Litster. In the event, and considering the circumstances, these men proved to be wise, competent and respected commanders.

The rebels both attracted and compelled support. By the

PREVIOUS PAGE Two of the rebel leaders of the Peasants' Revolt in conference, John Ball mounted, Wat Tyler on the left, identified by names written on their coats.

second week in June they were in control of Canterbury, and had looted the Archbishop's palace there, Their attitude was very much in tune with the ideals of the time: they were not purloining other people's property, they were righting wrongs. In effect they were reclaiming what had been taken from them in the first place. It was very much the Robin Hood spirit, and we will meet again this justification by appeal to a sense of rightness; it was an important underlying belief of the period.

In many ways the rebels showed themselves to be conservative in their thinking, and their loyalty to the Crown was a symptom of their assumptions about the inevitable chain of command. They themselves adopted forms of official government. Their aggression was against the tyrannical rich and the lawyers who enacted their extortions. This distinction, however, implied a degree of national disunity – the king seen as separate from the execution of the laws of the land and from the holders of power and wealth – which foreshadowed trouble for Richard.

Having organized themselves into a recognizable force, the rebels moved towards London. They travelled from Canterbury to Blackheath, reaching there by 12 June. At the same time a separate Essex force assembled at Mile End. The king moved from Windsor, not away from but towards the people's army, and took up residence, along with his chief advisers, in the safety of the Tower of London. The gates of the city were closed by order of the Mayor, William Walworth, who was to play a main part in the subsequent events.

In the meantime the most powerful and the richest citizen of the realm was noticeably absent. John of Gaunt was in the north, negotiating with the Scots, and on the arrival of the news of the outbreak of violence in the south he found himself isolated and vulnerable. His former confederate and friend the Earl of Northumberland no longer wished to know him. Clearly it was a time for playing safe. Gaunt with his private army could have hurried to the relief of the king, but instead he fled to Scotland, and remained in exile or sanctuary there until it was all over. Northumberland's swift change of loyalty – he refused to receive the Duke in his castles of Alnwick and Bamburgh – was a recognition of Gaunt's known unpopularity. Indeed he had good reason to know of this, since he

had been present in London when John of Gaunt had ignominiously been forced to flee the angry mob.

John of Gaunt's position was both dangerous personally and interesting politically. He did not have the full complement of his troops with him in the north, since they were at the time assembling at Plymouth under the command of his brother Edmund of Langley, preparing for an expedition to Castile to press Gaunt's claim to the Castilian throne. This example of the extent to which he felt able to pursue a foreign policy quite independent of the king's is a telling sign itself. But when the trouble broke out the army did not stir from Plymouth. Richard might well have wondered why not. Perhaps the Duke of Lancaster's faction may have considered that in the event of the unrest leading to Richard's deposition – as it happened a gross misreading of events – the likelihood of Gaunt's succession to the throne would best be increased by avoidance of involvement. What is clearly demonstrated by all this is the degree of disunity at the highest level in the state.

It was a Monday when the rebel army left Canterbury. By the Thursday they were outside the gates of London, and with some support already apparent in the city itself it was clearly time for action. The day was the feast of Corpus Christi, and the king, always correctly religious, heard mass at the chapel of the Tower of London. He then set out by boat together with his friend de Vere and several of his nobles. The idea was to cross the Thames and parley with the rebels near Rotherhithe, but the excited and numerous crowd which awaited him on the further bank was too much for the nerves of his companions. One gets the impression that Richard would have risked it, but he was in no position to insist against the trepidation of the others in the boat. The barge turned back and a futile attempt to carry on the discussion by shouting across the water seems to have made things worse. The king's party failed to explain to the rebels why he would not land to talk to them, and the intended conciliation collapsed largely through inaudibility. The king went back to the Tower.

This retreat stirred up the crowds to take precipitate action. They poured into Southwark, concentrating their anger on the way on the houses of the clergy, lawyers and court officials which filled the suburbs, including the Archbishop's hostel at

OPPOSITE The Chapel of St John the Evangelist in the White Tower, where Richard would have heard mass on the feast of Corpus Christi.

A scene from the crisis of the Peasants' Revolt. Richard's initial attempt to reach agreement with the rebels was made by boat. The unruly scene which faced him across the Thames prevented a landing, and the intention to parley failed.

Richard II sits in Council, surrounded by nobles and clergy.

Lambeth, later to become Lambeth Palace. How the gates of the city then came to be opened is not quite clear. There were undoubtedly sympathizers inside, and the rebels threatened to burn the city, thus presumably creating more support for their cause from the frightened London population. The Mayor, Walworth, and his council may well have decided that to let them in was the safest thing. Probably they saw that they had no option. Everybody then set about trying to appease them as they swarmed over London Bridge. They were plentifully supplied with food and drink, which by then they needed. Their first act was to open the prisons. Their second was to wreak revenge on John of Gaunt: they went straight to the magnificent Savoy Palace, and burned it down.

Froissart mentions that in this initial storm through the city a main target was the houses of foreigners, specifically Flemings and Lombards. These were probably picked as representatives of the alien rich, since the former were characteristically merchants and the latter bankers. By the Thursday evening the worst of the damage was done, and the rabble (as it had for a time become) quietened down. They drew together in St Catharine's Square, just below the walls of the Tower.

Tyler and his officers evidently reasserted their control, since the noise of the army then became more purposeful. Their demand was addressed to the Chancellor, that same Archbishop of Canterbury, Simon Sudbury, whose doings had rankled from the start. They wanted from him an account of the revenue raised during the last five years, implying that he would find the request embarrassing. Now the killing and burning was over, the underlying motive of tax grievance re-emerged.

Inside the Tower, meanwhile, there was disagreement. Walworth advised the king to mobilize an attack, relying on the rebels to fall into a drunken sleep later that night. No doubt they had taken care to pillage the cellars of the foreign merchants and bankers, and all the inns had been thrown open to them. One can imagine that the scheme would have worked: there were in London many powerful citizens, with sizeable vested interests in restoring order, who maintained their own armies of retainers. One of them, we are told, watched over his wealth with 120 armed men. But there was doubt about which side would be taken by the people of London themselves, and

OPPOSTE The magnificent panel portrait of Richard at his coronation occupies a prominent position opposite the west door of Westminster Abbey. It is thought to have been painted when he was in his twenties, though he looks appropriately younger.

the king was also given contrary counsel. 'Promise them everything they ask for', said the Earl of Salisbury. It is typical of Richard's methods that he took this advice.

Early on the Friday morning Richard arranged to meet the rebel leaders in person, but at a distance from the city, at Mile End. There he promised to listen to their grievances and grant their requests. Whether one of the demands which he conceded was the handing over of the hated ministers, or whether we should believe the alternative account by which Tyler, Straw and Ball broke into the Tower with a band of men as soon as the gates were opened to allow the king and his retinue to emerge, is still not clear. The latter version may have been an official invention to cover what would have been an act of gross treachery. A further alternative is that the leaders, negotiating with Richard at Mile End, temporarily lost control of the mob around the Tower.

In any case the rebels achieved one of their main aims: they took revenge on those they blamed for the unjust taxes. Archbishop Sudbury and the Treasurer, Sir Robert Hales, were seized and beheaded on Tower Hill. The heads were placed on London Bridge, like the heads of traitors. It was an act which might have damaged Richard's position, but instead the execution of an archbishop so shocked the people of London that the rebel cause began to lose popularity.

At the same time Richard promised to fulfil all the terms of the insurgents' demands. These closely reflected the sources of the problem, since they concerned rural wages and the occupation of land. Serfdom was to be abolished; land was to be rented at a fixed rate of fourpence per acre per year; payment for work was to be agreed by negotiation between the parties.

Richard showed for the first time at Mile End the streak of personal physical courage and even recklessness, the ability to surmount a crisis with coolness and mastery, which he may have inherited with his Plantagenet blood and which no doubt had been nurtured by his experience of the role and obligations of royalty. His followers quailed, and some turned back. Perhaps it was as well, since they were probably more unpopular, and less diplomatic, than he was. The king rode straight towards the vast crowd of country people, until he was actually among them. He addressed them in a friendly manner,

OPPOSITE The murder of the Archbishop Simon Sudbury shown here as taking place in the Tower of London, where he was seized. In fact he was beheaded on Tower Hill.

saying that he was their lord and king, and wished to know what it was they wanted. When they made their demands he agreed at once, promising to have letters made which would bear his Great Seal and guarantee the granting of their terms. He would send one of his banners with them to each of their places of origin. 'I will never go back on my word', he is reported to have said, though possibly with the stinging irony of hindsight: whatever his noble qualities may have been, and they were not insignificant, Richard consistently went back on his word.

The simple people cheered him. They had gained all they set out to get. It had been, they might have felt, suspiciously easy. But they were convinced. No doubt the promise of letters bearing the Great Seal and of the king's banners to take home impressed them. The writing of the letters began at once, and as they were delivered the country people began to go home. Richard had apparently triumphed.

He was only fourteen at the time. Again we are startled at this youthfulness, and have to make the sudden psychological adjustment to the notable precociousness of the Plantagenets. Richard's father was the victor of Crécy at the age of sixteen; his grandfather was king at fifteen, and launched the country into the Hundred Years War in his early twenties. Richard at fourteen seems to have been fully in control and able to make his own decisions.

When he returned to London he found that things were far from well. An immediate call on his attention was the plight of his mother, a woman now in her forties. She too had been in the Tower when it was broken into, and the unruly band, searching room by room for the Archbishop, had found her in her bedroom. Though they do not seem to have harmed her, they destroyed the bed, and frightened her so much that she fainted. She was quickly removed from the Tower by boat, and took refuge in another residence, the 'Queen's Wardrobe', near Blackfriars. There Richard joined her when he got back from the negotiations, and stayed with her the whole of the Friday night.

Tyler, Straw and Ball were not as easily put off as the simpler countrymen who had started home. The implication is that they had not (as apparently originally intended) been present at the Mile End meeting. They now stayed in London with a

OPPOSITE A miniature of Princess Joan, Richard's mother. During the crisis of the Peasants' Revolt Richard was concerned for her safety and arranged for her to be taken to Blackfriars after the Tower had been broken into by rebels in search of the Archbishop.

considerable body of supporters, and continued to stir up dissatisfaction in the city.

A further meeting was arranged for the next day, 15 June. On that Saturday morning Richard and his retinue first heard mass, as was his constant custom, this time in Westminster Abbey. It was a hot summer day in London, tempers were in any case on edge, and when the king's party rode out to Smithfield for the meeting many of them were sweating in concealed armour under civilian clothes. Froissart says the meeting took place by accident, as the king rode a roundabout way home; but this seems highly unlikely, since he must have known the whereabouts of the rebels. The fact that it consisted of a face-to-face confrontation with Tyler certainly indicates that it was arranged.

Wat Tyler emerges from the shadows now for his brief appearance in the centre of the stage of England's history. All this time we have known of him only as a name; now he takes on a character. It is not a pleasant sight, and Richard undoubtedly benefits by the comparison. But history is not written by peasants, and the historian is more likely to gain from the approval of kings. One would expect Tyler to have had a bad press, particularly in the years after his failure, but those reports, however partial, are all we have to go on.

Tyler's first action at Smithfield was to approach the king in the manner of an equal. The two met apart, each out in front of their respective parties. The peasants of course by far outnumbered the royal retinue: Froissart's figure of more than 20,000 versus sixty horsemen is unreliable, but nevertheless a guide to the disproportion. Instead of approaching humbly on foot, as a subject should, Tyler rode forward, bringing his horse aggressively close to Richard's. According to some reports the two then dismounted, and the rebel leader, instead of bowing, grasped the king's hand. He addressed him in terms which suggested equality, calling him 'brother', or simply 'King'. It was clear that his intention was to provoke a quarrel.

At first Richard was cautiously conciliatory. He acknowledged Tyler's command of the massive body of men; he assured him that the letters he had promised were all to be delivered. There was some slight delay caused by the individual drafting of them. But the matter was in hand.

Having failed to get a quarrelsome response from Richard, Wat Tyler turned his attention to his retinue. It is said that at this point he stirred some members of the king's party to anger by his uncouth manners. The tension of the situation and the hot June weather had made him dry, and he demanded water. He then 'rinsed out his mouth in a very rude and villainous manner before the King'. And this, apparently, was more than some people could bear. How it affected the fastidious Richard we do not know, but a heated exchange then took place between the rebel and one of the attendant squires. Possibly they were, as Froissart says, old enemies. Whichever one it was who started the dispute, the result, it is agreed, was that Tyler threatened to kill the squire. The whole matter has rather the style of a drunken brawl than of a royal parley.

The Mayor, the staunch William Walworth, then entered the argument. He accused Tyler of behaving improperly in front of his monarch – an understatement which shows a failure to understand the reality of the situation – and, perhaps at this indication that his dignity was affected, Richard lost his temper. From several pieces of evidence we know that he had that combination of control and passion which allowed him to remain calm after some would have exploded, but which erupted when the flashpoint was reached into the violence of suppressed fury.

He rinsed out his mouth in a very rude and villainous manner before the king.

Fired by the king's command to arrest the rebel, Walworth advanced, shouting abuse. He responded summarily and with the violence of anger to Tyler's resistance to arrest, flooring him with a blow of his large sword. The crowd around the fallen leader prevented the assembled peasants from seeing what went on. To the question passed among them, 'What is the king doing to our spokesman?' the reply came back, 'He is making him a knight' – an ironic error, given the supposedly revolutionary and egalitarian spirit of the revolt.

Once Wat Tyler was on the ground the anger of those around the king became uncontrollable. The mood of the day and the occasion was conducive to hitting a man when he was down, and Tyler seems to have had the knack of evoking personal loathing. A squire ran a sword into his stomach, and he died.

Things then looked for a moment decidedly ugly, and

OVERLEAF The rebel leader Tyler is struck down by one of Richard's attendants, and the king then finds himself confronted with the peasants' army, virtually alone. As always in moments of desperate crisis, Richard kept his head.

Everyday domestic scenes

A selection of illustrations from manuscripts:
BELOW LEFT A monk surreptitiously samples his wine
BELOW A man warms his feet in front of the fire
BOTTOM Scenes of meat preparation in a butcher's shop

LEFT The bakery. On the right bread is placed in the oven.

RIGHT A man on crutches passes a villager in stocks. Stocks were a well-used form of punishment and public ridicule.

RIGHT Milking a cow.

Richard showed once more his wonderful ability to think and act fast in a crisis. Crisis indeed it was, as the horde of peasants realized what had happened and surged forward towards the hopelessly outnumbered royal party. One of the chroniclers reports that at that point almost all his retinue deserted, leaving him virtually alone. The Crown and the royal person, and indeed much more, were for a few minutes in mortal danger. The common people were armed with their famed longbows, the very ones which had decimated French armies and become the terror of Europe. They had, it is said, actually started to shoot when the king rode out towards them.

His message, which he shouted, was a simple and effective one. Now that their leader had fallen, he, as their king, was their natural captain. If it is true that he put the argument in such terms, then it shows an accurate assessment of their spirit. Their cause was for king and commons, as against the lords, the clergy and officials. There were immediate signs that this tactic had worked, since some of the rebel army fell back. The Mayor, who had apparently remained near to his king, advised continuing to play for time. He probably knew that help would come, no doubt summoned by those who had fled back to the city. The king then pursued his initiative, and led his new rabble army further into the country, towards St John's Fields, an area of open-field agriculture where the corn crops were then standing green in the June sun.

Rather surprisingly, they followed their self-appointed leader. Military discipline among the rural people was, it seems, so thoroughly inbuilt, after those decades of war, that they instinctively obeyed an order. Meanwhile in London things were going as Walworth had hoped. Probably he had himself sent messages asking for support, and the effect was that among the prosperous citizens the rumour spread that the king was being killed, which, minutes before, had seemed likely to be the case. They were loyal, and they were themselves in danger, so their response was immediate and unequivocal.

The aldermen and powerful citizens gathered their forces, rode out, and surrounded the peasants in the open fields; some of the more militant wanted to attack, but the king advised allowing tempers to cool. He contented himself with recovering the letters and banners he had so far distributed, and allowing the mob to disperse. He intended to exact a full vengeance later. The policy of awaiting a favourable moment became typical of his politics, and it shows both coolness of calculation and strength of nerve. It had all been a trick, and it had worked. If Richard needed any confirmation of what was to be a major principle of his reign he had already, at this early stage, received it: deception pays.

The rebels threw down their bows and left, dispirited. The king made a triumphant entry into the capital, no doubt glad to be still alive. His first act was to comfort his understandably anxious mother. He had, he told her, recovered a kingdom which he had briefly lost. He must have been greatly encouraged, given the uncertainty of his own position, by the late display of loyalty on the part of the people of London. It is gratifying to hear that at the time of confrontation in the St John's Fields he had created a new knight, Sir William Walworth.

That same day official action was taken to clear London of the country people, and so intimidated had they become that they left at once. The two remaining leaders, Jack Straw and John Ball, were found and beheaded, and their heads, together with the dead Tyler's, were displayed on London Bridge, where the day before they themselves had put those of the unfortunate Archbishop and Treasurer. That had a powerful propaganda effect, and encouraged the dispersal.

It had been mainly a Kent and London event, but trouble had in the meantime broken out in several other parts of the country, as news spread of the initial success. Directed mostly towards local grievances, the scattered outbreaks lacked both the specific programme and the cohesion and organization which had at first aided Tyler's campaign. At St Albans and Peterborough and elsewhere in Cambridgeshire unrest broke out into violence, and there were pockets of disturbance in the Midlands. In Suffolk and Norfolk a more organized rising took place under the leadership of Geoffrey Litster, known as 'the king of the commons'. He too, however, was caught and executed. This Government wisely killed the rebel leaders at once, but most of the ordinary insurgents were allowed to go home unharmed.

As an attempt at revolution the peasants' rising had lasted less

Es nouvelles dAlbyon
Sil vous en plaist escouter

than a week, but its effects were to be as long and insidious as its causes had been. Yet for the time being nothing seemed changed. After 1381 the rural poor were apparently as powerless as they were before. A statute the next year decreed that the forced releases 'in the time of this last rumour and riot against the laws of the land and good faith shall be wholly annulled and holden for void'. The status quo was legally restored. Yet a new knowledge had been born: landlords now understood the danger of ignoring a smouldering discontent. The tension between the unions of resisting villeins and the exactions of the lords' courts continued. It must, however, have gone on in an atmosphere of greater caution on both sides. The process of the gradual decline of villeinage, which had been taking place for at least a decade before the revolt, took several generations to render serfdom obsolete. As a legal technicality it existed into the reign of Elizabeth I; it was economic and agricultural forces which finally destroyed it, not the force of arms.

A week to ten days after the dispersal of the peasants' force a royal army assembled at Blackheath. There were a few more skirmishes in Kent, and by the beginning of July Richard felt secure enough to revoke all his concessions of the Mile End meeting. He arrived in person at St Albans, and fifteen of the local ringleaders were condemned to death. The revocation of the agreed liberties was confirmed by Parliament in November, at which point also a general pardon was extended to those of the rebels not already killed in action or executed. Richard had proved his determination, his ruthlessness in retaliation, and his sense of timing. He had also taught the nation (to his own ultimate disadvantage) that he was a man whose word was not to be trusted.

The Tower of London, showing the White Tower with London Bridge in the background, from a fifteenth-century manuscript.

4 King, Court and Country

HE WAS a little under six feet tall; his youth and delicate features gave him a fragile medieval beauty, emphasized by the fresh complexion of his clear, pale skin; he wore his wavy fair hair long, below his ears but slightly above the collar. For most of his life he had neither beard nor moustache, though later in his reign he at one point adopted the probably unsatisfactory facial tufts of a fair-skinned person; he had long, artisic fingers, and small feet, encased in the modish pointed shoes of the time; he was also fashionably dressed.

Richard can be inspected by us now in several portrayals, including a manuscript illumination showing Jean Froissart giving him a book. In this depiction of an event which took place in the year 1395, the shoes of the king and court are almost ludicrously extended; pinched waistlines and skin-tight hose, together with the use of a sort of bowler hat perched right on top of the head, give to his companions a degree of foppishness approaching decadence, though the king wears a simple but striking scarlet gown. He looks politely pleased to be receiving the large dark volume with its gilded clasps. Froissart reports that though he was busy at the time with affairs of state he was cheerful and gracious in his manner, and talked to him cordially. We get the impression of extreme politeness, the product both of breeding and of natural ease. He dipped into the book at once, 'for he spoke and read French very well', and then had it taken to his private chamber.

The best portraits of Richard are in a panel and an effigy in Westminster Abbey, and in the 'Wilton Diptych', which hangs in the National Gallery. These works also have the advantage that they give us a clear feeling for the artistic style of the time.

The small scale of the Diptych, in particular, achieves a special tension between ornament and restraint, the delicacy of its portrayal of the figures contrasting with the richness of the gold background, the gold-pointed jewels, and the luxurious cloth-of-gold robe cloaking the king's body. The only prominent colour is a celestial blue which breaks out in the garments of the two king-saints who accompany him. Richard appears on the left-hand panel, a small figure kneeling below St John the Baptist (his patron saint), St Edward the Confessor, and St Edmund, king and martyr, quite dwarfed by these larger standing figures. In the other panel, by contrast much more

PREVIOUS PAGE Richard II presides over a banquet. Note the elaborate dishes and the extravagant ornamentation of costume and surroundings.

OPPOSITE Froissart presents a richly-bound book to Richard. The court dress is once again shown in its full modishness; the king however wears a simple scarlet gown. Froissart says he was gracious and friendly, and dipped into the book at once.

crowded, the Virgin and the infant Christ receive his prayers, surrounded by angels, all of whom are wearing his personal white hart badge, as if members of his court.

The king has a half-smile, a look of serenity and composure, his features, in the small and intricate painting, being clearly a personal portrayal by an artist who had seen him. The most striking features in the whole scene are Richard's long, fine fingers, protruding in supplication from his enveloping cloak.

The panel portrait, which faces visitors to Westminster Abbey as they enter by the West Door, is (in contrast to the highly delicate Diptych) large and confident, but nevertheless a work carried out with a certain fineness of touch. It is now rather obscured by its glass, but it is a firmly balanced composition in which the figure of the youthful king is framed by his considerable throne. Richard looks out at us, thoughtful and abstracted, his face bearing the expressionless vacancy of the portrait sitter. It is distinguished as being uniquely him, however, by the finely arched eyebrows and the bushy, curly hair. Once again we notice his thin, elongated fingers, here engaged in supporting his orb and sceptre. He is small in bone structure as well as in his youthfulness, and his rich clothes sit on him heavily.

The panel is thought to have been painted when he was in his twenties, but since it shows him in his coronation robes it probably intentionally made him look young. The Diptych also portrays a very young Richard, and also probably commemorates his coronation, though it too is thought to date from the mid 1390s.

The effigy was completed in 1397, and in it the king reposes with the young queen on his right. Richard now sports a small pointed beard and light moustache, and he lies heavily robed in fine gilt-bronze folds beside his queen, his hair and hers tied with headbands, below which Richard's breaks out into thick gold waves. His face, seen from beside the tomb in profile, is flat and bland, the nose, however, straight and surprisingly sharply pointed. A slight double chin proclaims approaching middle age, and we realize that we see here not the child king of the panel or the youth of the Diptych, but Richard in the period of his brief maturity.

The king lies now behind the High Altar, near his

magnificent grandfather Edward III, both occupying the side arches of the shrine of Edward the Confessor, founder of the great Abbey and one of Richard's most revered predecessors. Richard would clearly have been proud to rest in this place, housing as it now does the coronation chair and the Stone of Scone, together with the shield and the massive sword of Edward III. Such a reinstatement in death ironically proves him right in having maintained throughout his troubles the ultimate indestructibility of his royalty.

The delight which Richard displayed on being given a book was probably not just a matter of his willingness to please, though that undoubtedly existed. He genuinely loved books. He possessed a copy of the refined love story, the *Roman de la Rose*, a long French allegorical poem of the early fourteenth century, later translated into English, possibly partly by Chaucer; and his personal library included expensive editions of Arthurian tales of the knights Gawain and Perceval. The books

In the fine gilt-bronze effigy on his tomb in Westminster Abbey, Richard lies beside his first wife Anne. The tomb is situated at the back of the High Altar, in the shrine of Edward the Confessor. The effigy was made from life, and completed in 1397.

eius: gloriam quasi uni
geniti a patre plenum gra
ae et ueritatis. Amen.

were all fine things in themselves, bound in satin or velvet, with gilt studs and ornaments and golden clasps.

That life at his court was so much more sophisticated than at those of his father and grandfather was partly a result of Richard's own refinement and sensitivity. There is no doubt, though, that it drew considerable continental influence, both in its formality and its artistic bent, from his marriage to his beloved Anne.

Anne of Luxemburg was the daughter of Charles IV, king of Bohemia and Holy Roman Emperor. Both he and his father had fought against the English at the battle of Crécy, the latter dying in action. He, John of Luxemburg, king of Bohemia, was clearly a remarkable man. Though he was blind, he attended the battle in full armour, and insisted on taking part in the combat. Such an urge to prowess, amounting in fact to a mad obsession, is hard for us to understand. He had himself taken forward into the fight, and his loyal knights tied their horses to his in the press of the army so as not to lose him. The old king struck out bravely at the enemy, and the knights and their master died together, horses still tied, in a scene of tragi-comic pathos which can seldom have been equalled on Europe's battlefields. Charles the Emperor, however, displayed more sense of reality. When he saw the battle being lost, he left, and so survived.

However, such military, or un-military, activities, were by no means all that characterized the House of Luxemburg. Their court at Prague was a haven for craftsmen and artists of all sorts, and also the centre of imperial splendour and ceremony. When the daughter Anne came to London she brought with her a large household which, we gather from the styles which became typical of Richard's reign, may have included some of those artists. If indeed the influence of Prague came to England with Anne, with it came a much wider spread of European taste.

The House of Luxemburg had made a habit of artistic and literary patronage, which extended as far as Italy. European monarchy, as typified by them, was an international matter. Their other daughters, Anne's sisters, had all married into neighbouring dynasties. Anne's marriage with Richard was a familiar part of a pattern, though it is indeed surprising to find two traditional enemies becoming united. The House of

OPPOSITE A page from *The Hours of Anne of Bohemia* showing Anne and Richard.

Luxemburg, as their presence at Crécy demonstrates, were loyal supporters of the French crown, and Anne's aunt had in fact married the French king.

Other alliances had been promoted. There was hope in Italy that the English king would marry the heiress of the Visconti of Milan. Anne, however, was preferred by Richard's English advisers, and it turned out to be a marriage of love, though it produced no children. Had Richard died a normal death he would probably still have been heirless, so that the succession would in any case have proved disruptive. Anne was to die before him, in the early summer of 1394; with characteristic passion he had the part of the palace of Sheen where she died destroyed, demonstrating the strength of his affection for her. In her effigy on their joint tomb, in so far as one can see her where she lies on the far side of Richard, Anne appears round-faced in a pleasant, open way, with small features and long flowing hair, her young body constrained to a tight, flat, medieval figure. King and queen were exact contemporaries. When they married, on 14 January 1382, they were both fifteen.

It seems likely that Richard spoke English for preference – or Froissart would not have remarked with approval that he could speak French – but the court into which the continental queen arrived would have been fluently bilingual. One innovation at their court was the presence of large numbers of women, which was both an expense and a sign of the increased leisure and security that may have contributed to Richard's failure to see the storm-clouds approaching. It also no doubt led to greater culture and sophistication. There were dances and songs now, rather than jousts. Richard's father and grandfather might well have been surprised, perhaps even shocked.

If the clothes of the courtiers strike us as being over-stylized – with their tight hose, narrow, belted waist, flowing sleeves and padded shoulders, the outer gown ornamented with expensive jewellery – their diet indicates still more a luxurious, even indulgent, habit of life. Richard's chief cook published his recipes, which fortunately survive to give us a rare insight into the king's daily life.

The basis of the court cooking was a wine sauce flavoured heavily by spices, including oriental flavourings. Several of these sauces, mixing for instance sugar and ginger, must have

OPPOSITE An unusual portrayal of Richard, from a pictorial history of the kings of England, produced in about 1430.

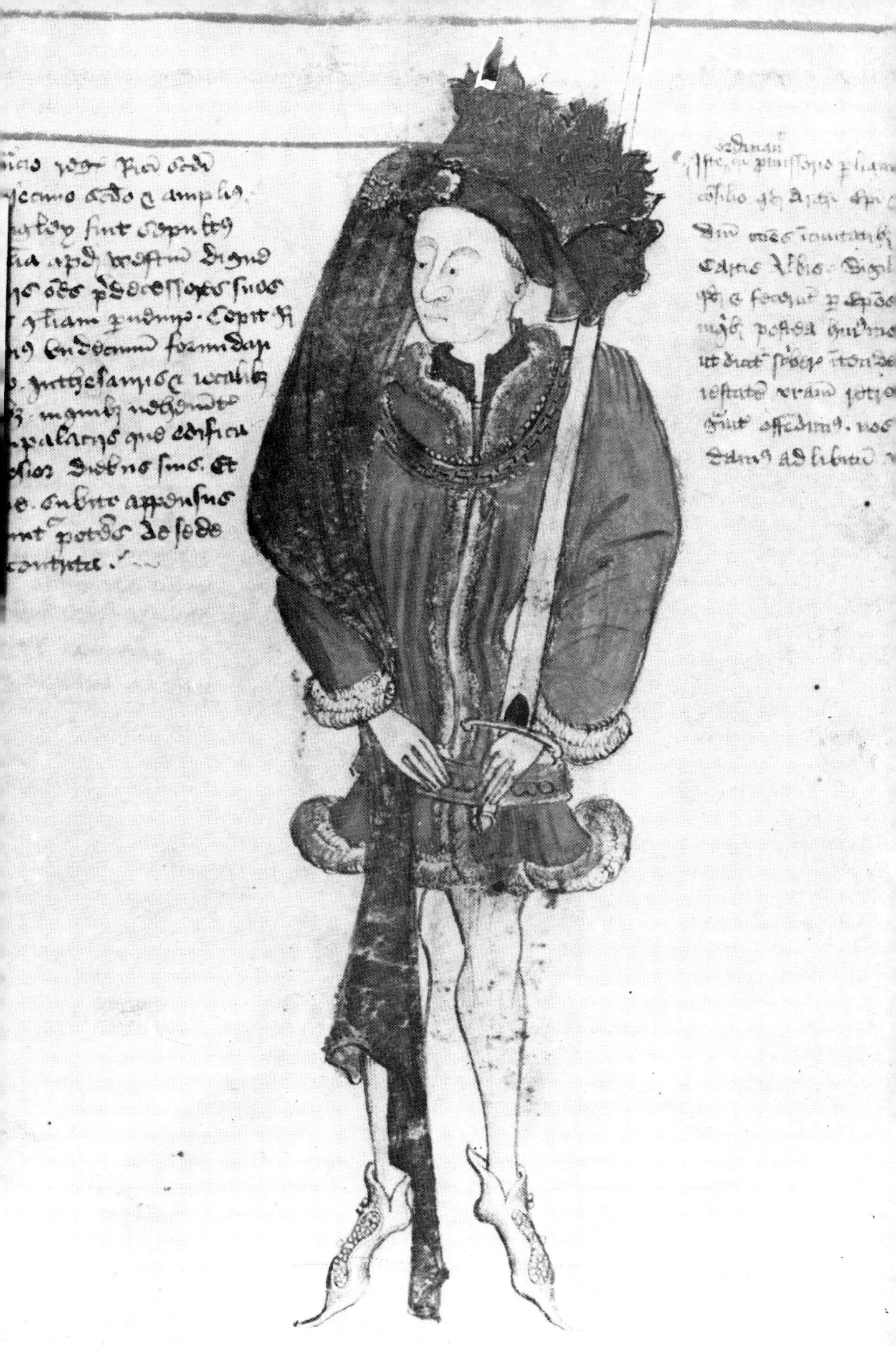

ABOVE A hunting scene in which a stag is hunted on foot with dogs. From a Bodleian Library manuscript.

LEFT AND BELOW These two views of life in the fourteenth century show its surprisingly sophisticated aspects. A customer buying mirrors in a shop views his face in one; and children watch a Punch and Judy show, a form of entertainment which has remained the same for centuries.

This scene from a fifteenth-century calendar gives an intimate view of domestic life. At this period the rich started having separate fireplaces in their chambers rather than using the communal hall or more public rooms.

been of a sweet-and-sour type. In a typical meal soup, such as venison broth, was followed by an elaborate central dish, perhaps minced pheasant with Greek wine sauce spiced with cinnamon, cloves and ginger. Oysters, again sometimes cooked in Greek wine, figured frequently, sometimes served on a bed of rice, again flavoured with sugar and ginger. All the dishes were highly dressed and combined: nothing was eaten plain. Hare pâté and deers' livers cooked in wine are among the simplest recipes.

Richard's passion for delicate and elaborate jewellery is another instance of his refinement and sophistication. The white hart theme, as brooch or badge, is everywhere; it was his mother's emblem, adopted as a sign of respect to her. One innovation which symbolizes the almost irritating fastidiousness emanating from the king was the invention of the handkerchief, which seems to have been for his personal use and took many years to pass into general acceptance: 'small pieces', says the wardrobe account in Latin, 'made for giving to the lord King for carrying in his hand to wipe and cleanse his nose.' Another equally notable innovation of this period was the cod-piece.

Court life started early in the day, and no doubt ended early, particularly at the darker end of the year. The midday meal, the main daily meal, took place at about eleven o'clock in the morning. It was followed by a time set aside for royal audiences; though if one can judge from one account it seems that Richard sometimes took an afternoon nap. Later in the afternoon they heard vespers, after which there were entertainments, then supper before bed.

The entertainments consisted partly of dances and songs, but the traditional Norman and French art of the minstrel was losing ground to a new and, as we shall see, important literary form: the serialized narrative poem. The author was replacing the performer. Fiction was in the process of becoming an independent field.

Court life was reasonably comfortable; the high-ranking nobles had their own suites of rooms. There was hot water, and fires were lit in the bedrooms; and another significant innovation by Richard was the private lavatory.

The king had four main palaces outside London, as well as the great state complex of Westminster. There was Eltham, which Edward III had made a royal palace, and which Richard had enlarged in the 1380s, with extensions to house his increasing court. There was King's Langley, used only for occasional visits, again enlarged during his ambitious building programme of the 1380s. Sheen (now Richmond) was a favourite, since it included a royal lodge, La Neyt, set in the privacy of an island. However, Edward had died there, and the queen's death there too perhaps convinced Richard (who we know was superstitious) of its bad fortune. Lastly Windsor Manor, a hunting lodge of Edward's, was in the process of being lavishly enlarged in the 1390s – Richard had spent £1,164 on it by his death – but was never completed. He left his second wife, the child Isabelle, there when he left for Ireland in 1399, never to return.

Westminster was something special and distinct from the courtly palaces, being the centre of administration. It included law courts as well as state apartments, and extended over a large and complicated area alongside the Abbey. There were halls – one named the White Hall, from which the street and area of that name derives – with splendid murals and decorations. Paintings of this period (the 1370s to the turn of the century) can still be seen, though in a poor state now, in the Chapter House of Westminster Abbey. Unfortunately the damaged and discoloured murals show us now only fragmentary faces, which give a tantalizing impression of a lively and expressive style. Biblical scenes are depicted with much medieval activity, a busy

OPPOSITE Richard largely rebuilt Westminster Hall in the 1390s. It shows now the new spirit of airiness and light which the Perpendicular style of architecture introduced.

crowded world full of Breughel-like characters verging on caricature. Tapestries were also much in vogue. Most striking of the Westminster complex of buildings was the Great Hall, which must have been, and indeed still is, the finest room in the land. It was rebuilt by Richard from 1393 onwards, and represents the time of architectural development when the Perpendicular style was reaching its definitive form. Gothic solidity is becoming lightened by a new airiness, a new mood of light and liberty.

The innovatory spirit directly stemming from the court and the royal couple at its centre spread in these several directions, and nowhere was it more apparent, or more long-lasting in its results, than in the realm of literature. Geoffrey Chaucer had been attached to the court of Edward III, and after Edward's death had remained in court circles through his connections with the household of John of Gaunt. He held minor offices and received an annuity, which may simply have been a recognition of his talents, and from time to time he played a part in the diplomatic exchanges of the time. He went to various continental cities with ambassadors, possibly acting as their secretary. In 1389 he became Clerk of the King's Works, and therefore theoretically responsible for Richard's great building programme taking place at that time. Richard's personal patronage of Chaucer testifies to the king's tastes and to Chaucer's prestige. But he evidently changed sides on Richard's deposition, as many in the country did, since we find him then being sponsored by Henry IV. There is even a possible indirect link with Richard's murder, since the man suspected of the deed was Chaucer's wife's nephew.

PREVIOUS PAGES The *Wilton Diptych* is a small and delicately painted pair of panels, now in the National Gallery. In the left hand panel Richard, kneeling, is supported by his patron saint John the Baptist and by the English national king-saints Edmund the Martyr and Edward the Confessor. In the right-hand panel we see the Virgin Mary and the infant Christ receiving Richard's prayers, surrounded by angels who bear his personal insignia of the white hart.

There is no danger of Chaucer's impact on English literature being underrated, since he has long been recognized as one of the great and seminal stylists of the language. It is perhaps not fair to compare him to Dante, although he admired and was much influenced by that master. Dante was dealing in deeper matters, in the medium of a higher style. Chaucer's poignant humanity is conveyed to us by means of something particularly, perhaps uniquely, English: that light edge of irony, the face so straight that those of a simpler frame of mind might well miss the fact that the tongue was in the cheek.

Chaucer wrote both about the conventional matters of his

century, classical allusions on the general theme of courtly love, and – here lies the innovation – of the bare reality of his time, in English, the language of the common people. That is not to imply that this was a new idea elsewhere, and indeed Chaucer himself was aware of the work of Boccaccio, whose Decameron had appeared in the 1350s. He made at least two trips to Italy, and possibly spoke Italian. What was new to English literature about the *Canterbury Tales* was the idea of telling a story in the vernacular for its own intrinsic amusement, rather than reworking in a skilful manner some traditional theme, or, more commonly, illustrating a moral or ideological message. Chaucer observed both these conventions at times, but they are not his trademark. It seems that the court of Richard II, with its lively interests, brought into being an environment in which the original creative artist, the author of fiction, could come into his own. Chaucer is busy satirizing the shortcomings of familiar, almost stereotyped, figures of his day; one might say that his purpose is social satire. And the poems certainly sparkle with epigrams and wise advice. But what his writing is in the end most concerned with is the fun of the thing itself, the process of literary creation, and the use of the supple and subtle Middle-English tongue to that end. We get the sense of the gleeful adventurousness of lively minds.

Chaucer was a man of the court, and his deflating of establishment figures was carried on, as it were, from the inside. We do, however, get an insight from his work not only into the tastes of those surrounding Richard but into the life of the classes within his reach outside the city. Chaucer led an active and wide-ranging life, and the view is likely to be accurate.

In the *Canterbury Tales* the clergy come in for a good deal of attention, and at times the good-humoured bantering tone slips towards bitterness, checked only by Chaucer's fundamental good nature. The ramification of the various orders and hierarchies, and indeed hangers-on, suggests an overweight institution. Bitterness about the wealth and non-productivity of the Church was undoubtedly a main theme of the late fourteenth century, underlying the great political tensions which are more accessible to the historian. But we get an insight too into other social movements, catching in the character of the Wife of Bath, for instance, a glimpse of an established

OVERLEAF LEFT This frontispiece from a manuscript now in Corpus Christi College, Cambridge, shows Chaucer reading his works. Recitals of serialized narrative poetry had begun to replace the art of the minstrel at Richard's court, a symptom of the artistic adventurousness of the time.

OVERLEAF RIGHT Two illustrations from a Bodleian Library copy of the *Roman de la Rose*, an early fourteenth-century French poem, a copy of which was included in Richard's own library. ABOVE A medieval castle with courtiers and knights. BELOW Love is invited to join the dance.

Characters from Chaucer's *Canterbury Tales*: ABOVE LEFT The Wife of Bath, ABOVE RIGHT The Miller, OPPOSITE LEFT The Knight and RIGHT The Pardoner.

burgess tradition, based on sufficient wealth to give security and practising the sort of respectability which, seen from a slightly different angle, is mild hypocrisy. We gain from Chaucer less feeling of the nuances of rural life: the yeoman, for instance, in the *Tales*, seems something of a stock figure. He is at his best with characters belonging to the bottom rung of the incipient middle class, such as the miller (the roughest member of the party), and the host. His basically comfortable characters are oblivious of the sufferings and resentment which had so recently caused the Peasants' Revolt.

Chaucer's friend and immediate contemporary John Gower was of even more substantial standing, a man of apparently independent means who belonged, as writer, to the mainstream of courtly poetic tradition. Yet he too was inspired by the originality of thought of this particular time, and his poetry reveals the sort of initiative which would not have been possible in circumstances less intellectually stimulating. It seems that he came from Kent, where he owned land, and was thus personally affected by the Peasants' Revolt. Though his minor writings

have a decidedly traditional ring, the inclusion of political opinions in the *Vox Clamantis*, first published in 1390, is striking and informative. We know that Gower, too, was connected both with Richard's court and with the household of John of Gaunt, and it seems that his contact with the Lancastrian party encouraged him (like Chaucer, only more blatantly) to adopt a flexible allegiance.

The *Vox Clamantis* was written in Latin, and may therefore be supposed to be for the ears of those in power. It is surprising, therefore, to find that it is overtly political, and critical of both Government and Crown. The first quarter of it is a description of the Peasants' Revolt, in which the clergy and the upper classes in particular come in for blame. The king himself is exonerated in the early edition – 'The boy himself is blameless, but his councillors are not without fault ...' – but with Gower's changing opinion, and perhaps the already visible symptoms of Richard's coming downfall, later editions shift the blame to Richard himself: 'The king, an undisciplined youth, neglects the moral acts by which he might grow from a boy to a man ... O

king, do away with the evils of thy reign, restore the laws and banish crime; let thy people be subject to thee for love and not for fear.'

Gower, in fact, both foresaw the coming trouble, and committed himself to his recognition of it. We know that he was personally known to the king. He tells us how he was on the river one day and encountered the royal barge, which Richard invited him to board. He suggested then that Gower should write 'some new thing', and the result was the English-language poem *Confessio Amantis*. It is conventionally didactic and on the traditional theme of love, but the fact that it is in English shows a modernistic attitude no doubt directly influenced by the popularity of Chaucer. The king had in effect commissioned the work, and no doubt he would have read it. Yet in some copies at least a first dedication to Richard was erased in favour of one to Henry Bolingbroke, perhaps as early as 1391; a step which shows both courage and foresight.

Confessio Amantis manages to include within its tale of love much social criticism, and of a pessimistic nature. Clearly the Peasants' Revolt had dispelled none of the national dissatisfaction. Only in an ideal world such as the one in which Orpheus played could real social harmony exist:

> Alswel the lord as the shepherd,
> He brought them all in good accord
> So that the common with the lord
> And the lord with the common also
> He sette in love bothe two . . .

While Chaucer showed a certain middle-class complacency, Gower was sharply critical of the social and political reality, though from a strictly intellectual point of view. It is possible that the differences in political awareness between the two poets led to a break in their friendship, for which there is some evidence in the texts. But we hear the cry of pain and indignation at first hand when we turn to William Langland. Where Gower's comments are overt and intentional, Langland's tend to make their point by implication, and are if anything the more telling for that.

While the other two were writing in the immediate aftermath of the Peasants' Revolt, William Langland composed

OPPOSITE The *Liber Regalis*, a valuable possession of the Dean and Chapter of Westminster Abbey, is thought to have been specially made for the coronation of Anne, Richard's queen. The frontispiece shows Richard himself in the coronation chair.

Piers Plowman immediately before it; and what is really striking from this evidence is that that desperate upheaval seems to have made absolutely no difference. Like the peasants' leader John Ball, Langland was an unbeneficed clergyman, and he shows Ball's tendency to pin the blame largely on the rich clergy – a sentiment which even Chaucer, from his less critical position, would have applauded. *Piers Plowman*, which the author continuously revised, we may regard as belonging largely to the 1370s. It is written in a West Midlands dialect, and is staunchly traditional in form, that is, it is a true medieval allegory, a moral fable – set, however, in the very real context of fourteenth-century England.

Some laboured at ploughing and sowing. . . . Others spent their lives in vanity.

It is a land in which 'some laboured at ploughing and sowing, with no time for pleasure, sweating to produce food for the gluttons to waste. Others spent their lives in vanity, parading themselves in a show of fine clothes.' The king is still in his minority, and John of Gaunt appears as a figure of fear, allegorized in a story about a cat. Meanwhile Piers advises a knight not to ill-treat his tenants or ill-use his serfs, echoing Ball's theme by adding that all are the same in the eyes of God. 'It is very hard to tell a knight from a serf when he comes to lie in the church-vaults.' The figure of Hunger looms over the lives of the country people. Yet part of their problem arises from their expectation of higher wages, to which the prospect of independence from Hunger has given rise. Once again one of our sources happily confirms another, and here we have a direct counterpart to Froissart's analysis that it was the increased prosperity of the common people, not their increased poverty, that brought about the rising. We see demonstrated at first hand the historian's identification of one of the causes of the revolt. The labourer grows angry unless he gets high wages; he curses the king and his council for making statutes, as if these were intended to plague the working people. Yet

> Whiles hunger was her maister: there wolde none of hem chyde,
> Ne stryve ayeines his statut: so sternilich he looked.

Langland gives us a view of the world outside the court, and it is a world of changing times. The rich are tending to abandon their traditional obligations to the poor: they economize on their households, and instead of feasting in the great hall they eat

OPPOSITE This tavern scene is taken from a fourteenth-century treatise on the Seven Deadly Sins. The style, approaching caricature, is typical of the explicit and detailed illustration of the time, as may be seen in the remnants of murals in the Chapter House of Westminster Abbey.

The beheading scene from the tale of *Sir Gawain and the Green Knight*. The mysterious knight picks up his severed head and challenges Sir Gawain to a return combat.

by themselves in a private room 'with a fireplace of its own'. There is much talk of the need to give generously to beggars, from which we sense both a real state of poverty and growing awareness of deprivation.

Yet to cite these cases of social consciousness on their own would give a false picture of the values of the world in which Richard and his contemporaries lived. The anonymous author of *Sir Gawain and the Green Knight* and of *Pearl*, for instance, accepted the ancient ideals of knighthood and of knightly conduct which supported a more traditional and less realistic mode of life. These ideals, we may suspect from their behaviour, lay as hidden assumptions behind the acts of some of the men of power. They are exemplified too by the work of the 'Chandos Herald', who glorified the adventures of the Black Prince in 'unknown lands'. The tension between the reality and the ideal must always have been present in the conscience of thinking people at this mature period of the Middle Ages, and the king himself must have been torn as much as anyone by the conflict of past hopes with present facts.

Ideal standards of personal loyalty, such as that which motivated Sir Gawain, together with romantic concepts of friendship and adventure in a wild world symbolized by the great forest, began in our period to be undermined by political and economic complexity. We have already seen and will see again that the ideal aim of the gaining of glory by fearlessness and by prowess in combat, and particularly by the relentless pursuit of justice, was far from dead. Might should be used in the promotion of right. The black and white contrast of right and wrong could still compete with the established law, the official will of Parliament or of the Crown. Though figures such as Tyler directly conflicted with the view that all behaviour should be governed by courtesy and a sense of one's role, yet for some a feeling of absolute duty to one's immediate lord remained supreme. In the final revolution the alignments of the Nevilles and the Percys showed an acceptance of the superiority of such demands to any feeling of centralized power. The king could, in such terms, be fallible. And no doubt Bolingbroke's claim to be pursuing his just rights did much to draw to him the support of those who still believed such conventions to be superior to any claims the monarch might have to absolute power based on divine authority.

In all this Richard himself remains in that position of ambiguity which we may regard as his trademark. If his upbringing and experience had given him the feeling of prerogative which was later to be formalized as the divine right of kings, this was in tune neither with the received traditions of his time nor with the practical reality. Perhaps it is inevitable that somebody at such a focal point of tensions should find himself frequently out of step. But perhaps too his position is part of the consequence of an inbuilt conflict between the two

Pilgrims in the fifteenth century. Pilgrimage was a fashionable occupation in Richard's time, and led to the dissemination of information and opinion.

contexts: the ideal and the real. As so often with systems of ideals, the supposedly rigid set of rules was relied on sometimes and at other times blithely ignored. But it certainly does not seem to have had much governing force over the king himself.

It is Richard's temperament as much as anything which sets him apart from his background. During his career we find a growing loss of self-control which some have seen as increasing neurosis. Whatever the cause, the king's actions departed more and more from the notions of gentleness and good manners which were associated with nobility. His father, for instance, is described as personally serving the king of France at table when he was prisoner after Poitiers, on the grounds that he was unworthy to sit at the same table as so great a prince and so brave a soldier.

Richard, however, dealt imperiously and impetuously with those he clearly regarded as his inferiors. He dismissed his Chancellor, Richard Scrope (or le Scrope), in 1381, for hesitating to carry out a dubious instruction to commandeer the Earl of March's estates on his death. He wrote in terms of outright anger to the commissioners at Devizes when they dared to assert their independence in making grants. He publicly insulted the Earl of Arundel when the latter criticized his policies. After a quarrel with his uncle, John of Gaunt, he actually ordered his summary execution, causing the Duke to ride to Sheen with armed support, which show of strength led to a tense reconciliation. Most striking is his anger at Archbishop Courtney, who warned him then that the high-handed treatment of Lancaster might be seen as a threat to the other great magnates. Richard went so far as to draw his sword, obliging his attendants to restrain him from the crime of murdering the Archbishop. In more understandable circumstances he flew into a rage at the funeral of Anne his queen, imputing to the Earl of Arundel an intended insult to the deceased in arriving late, and hit him with such force that he knocked him to the floor and drew blood – all this in the conspicuous exposure of Westminster Abbey. In strict medieval terms a monarch could not, however greatly put upon, deal in such crude ways with nobles of his realm.

The point is that such behaviour, performed in public, was as explicit a flouting of chivalrous convention as anything that Wat Tyler had done. It cannot but have led to both distrust and disrespect in those around him.

5 An Insecure Throne

To UNDERSTAND Richard's position one has to realize that at that period a handful of the more powerful nobles would think it their natural right to influence, even to control, the king. Traditionally both parties collaborated in a sort of working relationship in which his duty was to take account of their interests. If their expectations had been increased by Richard's minority, the fulfilment of them was to find itself thwarted by his personal wilfulness.

Another element in fourteenth-century politics which tended to display a mind of its own was Parliament, which had already established itself in the role of controlling, through the legalizing of taxation, the flow of funds to the Government. Edward II had formulated the system of summoning representatives from the shires, and by the end of the reign of Edward III a firm two-chamber structure was in existence. The Lords, still the highest authority and the ultimate legal power, frequently needed (and sometimes failed) to obtain the support of the Commons, the assembly of knights and burgesses which represented a broader interest. King and Lords in collaboration could cow the Commons into acquiescence. King and Commons could combine to thwart the Lords. But what fatal grouping for the Crown would arise if Lords and Commons pooled their interests against it. There is nothing like the holding of purse strings as a means of governing behaviour.

Conflicts between Richard and Parliament had started early. In 1382 a seemingly high-handed move on his part to transfer the Mortimer estates to members of his Household on the death of the Earl of March in 1381 had drawn, as was mentioned in the last chapter, dubious hesitation from Sir Richard Scrope, the Chancellor. Richard dismissed him impetuously, an act which the chronicler Walsingham points out was unconstitutional, because Scrope was the appointee of Parliament, not of the Crown. This led to fears on the part of others in power that the young king would tend to assert personal preference, rather than to act within the form of regular government, which was more subject to their control.

There were from then on four chamber officials whose rise to power and wealth under personal royal patronage formed a threat to those who traditionally expected such favours. They were the new Chancellor, Michael de la Pole, the Chamberlain,

PREVIOUS PAGE The arrest of the Duke of Gloucester. The Duke is escorted to a boat to be taken into exile, while the king and his young supporters complacently ride away.

Robert de Vere, the under-Chamberlain, Sir Simon Burley, and the Receiver of the Chamber, John Beauchamp. Their posts and their closeness to the king signalled a form of chamber government which would prove hard to infiltrate. Robert de Vere's close personal relationship with Richard was demonstrated by a blatant lavishness in the bestowal of property, and this in itself must have reminded many of the treatment of Gaveston by Edward II. Richard's public display of emotion when, later, de Vere's body was brought back from his death in exile for reburial was to confirm that his favouritism had a more than political aspect. Simon Burley, a confederate of Richard's father, had acted as tutor to him during his childhood, and although his experience and age must have made him a sound adviser, he used his new position of privilege to indulge in ostentatious displays of wealth, which must have been almost as provoking to the magnates as his power and influence over Richard. He too gained lands and offices, and grew to become one of the land's wealthiest citizens. The rewards with which Richard recognized (and kept) the loyalty of these men were precisely of the sort – the granting of territory – which the magnates would have felt to be their own exclusive right.

Trouble in Scotland, the need for a French campaign and for increased defences resulting from the threat of invasion from the Low Countries, brought into prominence the question of royal finances. Parliament in the meantime grew increasingly restive during the early 1380s. In February 1383 the Commons asked the king to arrange to bring his Household expenses under control. In October the Lords complained about his bad advisers. In the Parliament of April 1384, after further difficulties in Scotland, the Earl of Arundel launched an outspoken attack on the king's policies. Bad leadership was threatening danger to the nation. Richard's famous display of temper followed, and John of Gaunt rashly intervened in an attempt to pacify his nephew. The king's anger was then drawn on to him, a situation complicated by a rumour that Gaunt was plotting treason. This in turn was followed in 1385 by a possible plot against Gaunt himself by the king's young supporters, which led to a direct quarrel between the king and his uncle. The Archbishop of Canterbury and other lords complained, and the angry confrontation at an accidental meeting on the river, when Richard apparently attempted to kill Canterbury, was the uncomfortable outcome.

An expedition to Scotland led to further tension between Richard and Gaunt, the king seemingly distrusting the Duke's motives. The ever-present dangers of both Scotland and France were highlighting the continuing need for money, when events in the Iberian Peninsula led to Gaunt's leaving to take the opportunity to press his Castilian claim in July 1386. Meanwhile the Parliament of October 1385 had granted a subsidy, which was used partly to finance Gaunt's expedition. And at that Parliament the Lords and the Commons had united to condemn the king's extravagance, his misuse of patronage and the impoverishment of the Crown by lavish gifts. Richard had no option but to allow a survey of his revenues by a commission. This demand, however, was for a time ignored by the Chancellor, de la Pole, notably the king's man.

The Parliament of October 1386 was controlled by the opposition, and it should have been plain to Richard that he was in definite danger. He had in the meantime continued to act without any sense of tact, elevating his friend de Vere in December 1385 to the rank of Marquess (a title created for this purpose), which had the significant effect of raising him above the Earls. He chose the worst possible moment to take the next step in this programme of dangerous defiance, by creating de Vere Duke of Ireland in October, the month that fatal Parliament sat, in 1386.

Dukedom was traditionally restricted to members of the royal family. There had so far been only one exception to this rule, and that was the ennoblement of one of Edward III's most powerful citizens. At the start of Edward's reign the only Duke in England was the king himself, as Duke of Aquitaine, and he set a precedent by creating his son the Black Prince Duke of Cornwall. Gaunt became Duke of Lancaster, Lionel Duke of Clarence, and in 1385 followed the elevation of Edward's remaining descendants when Edmund Langley became Duke of York and the youngest son, the Earl of Buckingham, was created Duke of Gloucester.

That act itself, however, was an uncomfortable comparison to de Vere's dukedom of the following year. It had always been understood that titles were accompanied by appropriate

Justice and its outcome is illustrated in this scene from a French fifteenth-century manuscript. Legal debate and appeal to legal opinion were replacing the traditional recourse to combat.

territory, to give a revenue from land, and certainly this was the case with the elevation of Richard's close associates. But Gloucester received instead an annuity of £1,000 drawn from the customs, and hence under the king's control. He had also suffered a further financial and dynastic blow, by having his hopes of the Bohun inheritance thwarted by John of Gaunt. Gloucester had married the co-heiress, and since her sister was at the time a nun had hopes to succeed to their valuable possessions of the earldoms of Hereford, Essex and Northampton. But John of Gaunt had the other heiress removed from her convent and married to his son Henry Bolingbroke, Earl of Derby.

Robert de Vere was an earl himself, and so not negligible. But the magnates clearly looked down on him, presumably because his inheritance had dwindled to the extent of leaving him comparatively poor when he entered Richard's court. His father, Froissart reports them as saying, was never a man of high reputation. 'It was always the case that when a poor man rises in the world and receives honour from his master, he grows corrupt.' Base men cannot resist the spoils of fortune: 'What good can come of this intimacy between the Duke of Ireland and the King?'

There was yet a further reason for personal animosity between Gloucester and de Vere. The latter had married one of the king's cousins, Gloucester's niece. In 1387 he left her for a foreign attendant of the queen's. The gulf between Richard and his uncles was significantly widened.

A deputation from Parliament to Eltham (where the king remained, refusing at first to attend the sitting) demanded the dismissal of de la Pole. Richard replied with a famous message that he would not dismiss even one of his scullions at Parliament's command. The witticism was evidently not appreciated. It seems that a direct threat of deposition may then have followed, and Parliament's demands were met. De la Pole was impeached and imprisoned. A Commission of Government was then set up, including Gloucester, the Earl of Arundel and his brother Thomas, Bishop of Ely, which was to have full control of government and power over the king, and in return for these immense concessions its life was limited to one year.

It was always the case that when a poor man rises in the world and receives honour from his master, he grows corrupt.

Freed from a direct role in governing his country, deprived of his seals, and under immediate threat of the inspection of his Household finances, Richard took evasive action by going on progress. Messages continued to flow between him and the Council, they perhaps being more concerned to know what he was up to than he was to collaborate with them. It was thought that he was planning to negotiate peace with France, and in view of future actions it seems likely that he had already thought of enlisting the former enemy's help. In August 1387 he took the interesting step of investigating his legal position, by applying to the courts of King's Bench and Common Pleas to know whether the setting up of the Commission was within the law.

The lawyers responded unambiguously in his favour. The royal will was not to be coerced. Finding themselves illegal had no doubt a powerful effect in impelling the Lords to firmer action. The Commission was due to expire on 19 November 1387, and it is probable that the legal decision, with its implications of treason, led its members to fear their subsequent arrest. On 14 November they published an 'appeal of treason' against five of Richard's central councillors – de la Pole, de Vere, Neville, Brembre (or Bramber), former Mayor of London, and Tresilian, the Chief Justice. From this, the mainstay of their case, they came to be known as the Lords Appellant. Led by Thomas Woodstock, Duke of Gloucester, Edward III's seventh and youngest child, these Appellants consisted at first of the Earl of Warwick, Thomas Beauchamp, and Richard Fitzalan, Earl of Arundel. They were later joined by Henry Bolingbroke, Earl of Derby, and the king's former friend and associate Thomas Mowbray, Earl of Nottingham. Mowbray had probably turned against the king through jealousy at the greater success of de Vere's friendship. The involvement of Derby associated the Lancastrian party with the revolt, and must have had a constraining influence on Gloucester's ambitions, since with Gaunt absent only the presence of his son would deter any thoughts Gloucester might have had about the throne.

The appeal was repeated to Richard personally in Westminster Hall on 17 November. De Vere was in the meantime raising an army in Cheshire and North Wales, and Richard played for time. He referred the matter to Parliament. It was an astute move, and it gave two of the accused, de la Pole and Neville, a chance to escape abroad. De Vere then marched with about 4,000 men towards the Severn valley. The Appellants were forced to accept a confrontation, and in due course the two armies met, late in December, at Radcot Bridge, on the Thames in Oxfordshire. De Vere, who was evidently no tactician, was easily beaten, the battle turning quickly into a rout. He himself escaped and fled abroad, to die in exile five years later.

The victorious Appellants entered London, receiving support from the citizens, took the Tower and with it the king. Richard, captured on about 27 December, was temporarily virtually deposed. It seems that the two younger Appellants exercised a restraining influence, and Richard wisely played on

The courts of inner temple

With the growing respect for legalism came increasing power for the judiciary. These illustrations from an early fifteenth-century manuscript show the different courts of justice. FROM LEFT TO RIGHT The Court of Common Pleas, The Court of Chancery and The Court of the Exchequer.

their detachment from the Gloucester faction. It is said that he dined with them that night. No doubt he fully appreciated the importance of using Derby's role as representative of the Lancastrian party against his uncle's attempts at power. The absent John of Gaunt must now have seemed a welcome friend.

The Appellants were, however, determined to press home their advantage. Richard was not permanently deposed, but he was for the time being powerless. The reference of the case to Parliament, however, was unassailable, particularly as the Appellants owed much of their success to their ability to ally themselves to the Commons. Parliament was called for February the next year, and they had to wait.

We have a good description, by the 'Monk of Westminster', who was probably present, of the 'Merciless Parliament' of February 1388. It was held in the White Hall of Westminster Palace, with Richard himself on the throne and the Chancellor, Thomas Ardundel, Bishop of Ely, on the Woolsack. The hall was packed, and the five Appellants entered it last, together. The document of appeal was a long French text which took two hours to read. It was careful not to lay the blame directly on the king, but instead accused his advisers, especially de Vere. No doubt the previous court ruling still gave rise to fears of accusations of treason, which in the event were to prove justified. There was some display of loyalty to Richard. The document's legality was questioned by the lawyers, and the Appellants were forced to resort to the House of Lords, as being the higher court and above the Civil Law – an early sign, it is sometimes said, of the move towards the supremacy of Parliament.

The debate in the House of Lords took a week, and resulted in rather doubtful support for Gloucester and his appeal. The case, however, was still pressed. The only accused present was Nicholas Brembre, the ex-Mayor of London, who put up a worthy defence. The Chief Justice Tresilian, however, was then found in hiding, and executed. Legal means having failed, Gloucester and his party resorted, undeterred, to the rule of might. Brembre had some support, but the city was at the time divided between rival guilds, the victuallers and the drapers, and no clear majority could be found for or against him. But they executed Brembre anyway, and the act was made to seem all the more guilty by the long-drawn-out failure to make it appear legal.

It was mid-March by the time the Appellants moved on to the main target of their attack. They abandoned their technique of appeal, and resorted to direct impeachment. Several executions followed, and the judges who had found the Commission illegal were banished to Ireland. Also banished was the king's confessor. The offensive was approaching uncomfortably close to Richard, and indeed the time came when the impeachments reached his personal Household.

Four of his chamber knights were charged, including Sir Simon Burley. Their main case against him, it seems, is that he had misused his influence over the king. There was also, according to Froissart, a rumour that he had been exporting wealth, in the form of gold and silver, to a personal hoard in Germany, using his constableship of Dover Castle to get it secretly out of the country. The Commons were against him, at any rate, and the viciousness of the Appellants' determination to destroy him requires some explanation. Such perhaps is furnished by an accusation that he had been involved in a plot to assassinate the members of the Commission. That, on the other hand, may well have been a face-saving measure to cover a desire to deprive the king of his closest advisers. It must have been a bitter blow for Richard, and brought home to him even more forcefully than all the previous events his ultimate powerlessness.

Burley was found guilty and condemned to death. Bolingbroke and Mowbray, separating themselves from their colleagues, pleaded for his life. Richard himself pleaded strenuously. Even his other uncle, the Duke of York, joined the cry for mercy. Richard so stretched his royal dignity as to allow Anne, his queen, to go on her knees in tears before Gloucester. But the three principal Lords Appellant were unrelentant. They had the security of knowing that the people were on their side, and that the ultimate threat of a popular rising was more than their opponents were prepared to face. Burley was executed on 5 May.

The Commons, demonstrating their approval of (or control by) the Appellants, awarded them £20,000 for 'their great expenses in serving the kingdom'. Gloucester acquired, from

Coins of the reign of Richard II: the Gold Noble and the Noble.

the forfeitures arising from the sentences of the Merciless Parliament, the territory which he had lacked. The main justification for the whole exercise, however, had been the need to put the royal affairs in order, and this was to some extent done. Some of Richard's debts were paid, and steps were taken to control his Household with a view to avoiding further insolvency. The process also robbed him of any sort of personal power. The Household was no longer the strong political force it had been, and he found himself subject to the close supervision of the committee of magnates.

In spite of all this Richard was by no means beaten. How exactly he achieved a situation in which he could restore himself to a position of direct control remains slightly mysterious, but the fact is that he did. The circumstances must have had a great deal to do with the relationship between the Commons and the Appellants, and the extent to which the latter's conduct of affairs failed to satisfy the former.

The war with France had continued, Gloucester's and Arundel's policy being to pursue aggression. But a subsidy voted by the Merciless Parliament proved to be inadequate, and the campaigns lacked success. At the same time the Scottish attacks intensified – the rival demands on resources by now being only too familiar – and an invasion of the summer of 1388 ended in disaster for the English. Henry Percy, son of the Earl of

Northumberland and known as Hotspur, was captured at the battle of Otterburn. The English fleet, which could have come to the rescue, was in action under Arundel on the coast of France, and there was no help for the northern nobility from the Appellants' Government.

Parliament sat on 10 September at Barnwell Priory in Cambridge, the only time an English Parliament has been held in that city. Richard was now alone, bereft of his close advisers, but also significantly freed by their absence both from their over-strong influence and from the effect of their unpopularity. The Commons had two main complaints against the rule of the Appellants: the war was unsuccessful and expensive, and at home the country was suffering from the disorderly conduct of bands of liveried retainers maintained by the magnates. These particularly rankled with the shire knights who, while being unable to afford small private armies of their own, suffered, or stood to do so, by such activities on the part of their powerful neighbours. What amounted to private police forces put to the use of furthering private ends stood in place of any secure national system of order.

Richard was able to exploit both these sources of tension. His well-known willingness to negotiate with the French promised peace and hence, most significantly to the Commons, lower taxation. And he too had an interest in curbing the freedom of magnates to maintain liveried bands, which competed undesirably with the Crown's own retinue with its insignia of the white hart. It is this concern with the exploitation of livery that is stressed by the Westminster chronicler as being the main business of this Parliament.

Richard made the striking move of offering to abolish all liveries, including his own. Although this was not allowed by the Lords, it must have had crucial appeal to the Commons. There was delay – again instigated by the king – in taking any positive action, and by 1389 a new factor entered the balance of power. John of Gaunt was due to return soon from Aquitaine. At earlier times a threat in his own right, he now took on the role of counter-threat to Gloucester, and when he finally arrived home that autumn Richard's ingratiating behaviour was clearly symptomatic of his awareness of the need to play one power-group against another.

In the meantime Richard took a surprising step. The Council met at Westminster in January, and after some initial hesitation, which may well have been due to his customary habit of playing for time, he met it in person on 3 May. The security of his position can only be explained to history by all the factors outlined above, but to the Council itself it came as a great surprise. He announced his majority, and his decision to govern the country by himself. 'I am of full age to govern myself, my household, and my realm, for it seems wrong to me that I should be treated with less consideration than the meanest of my subjects.' For twelve years he and the country had been subject to the rule of others, and the result had been heavy taxation. With his personal policy of peace he would bring prosperity. It is a message often repeated by political parties seeking power and, as so often subsequently, it succeeded.

The Chancellor, Thomas Arundel, was dismissed. So were the Treasurer and the Keeper of the Privy Seal. Gloucester and the Earl of Arundel were temporarily excluded from the Council. Significantly, Bolingbroke's position on the Council was retained. Richard asserted power of appointment of the judiciary, and he there and then embarked on ten years of uninterrupted personal rule.

The years between can be seen either as a period of success or as the germination of the seeds of decline; it depends whether one views them in relation to the past or to the future. Much took place, as we shall see, both at home and abroad. Before we go on to view Richard's career and the state of his country in this period of his personal reign, and to see the way it led inevitably and with accelerating speed to his deposition, this is the natural point at which to tell the end of the story of the troubles of 1386–8, the sequel to the revolt by the Lords Appellant.

It is typical of Richard both that he could bide his time, and that when the chance eventually came for him to take revenge he showed that his resentment was undiminished. Apparently it took him ten years to build up sufficient confidence.

Froissart describes the state of tension at the court in the mid-1390s. Gaunt was back in Aquitaine from 1394, and Gloucester was an unwelcome presence at the Council. Richard had succeeded in surrounding himself again with younger nobles, who may well have influenced him to believe in Gloucester's

Charles VI of France, father of Richard's second wife Isabelle.

disloyalty. Froissart describes Gloucester as plotting to turn the people of London against the king. Above all, no one had forgotten the execution of Simon Burley.

In January 1397 Richard found himself criticized by the Commons for the extravagance of his Household, a situation which must have seemed ominously familiar. The question of liveries had still not been satisfactorily settled, and he made further promises to control their use. But in reply to the accusation of undue expense he brought into play the Lords, who judged that such accusations were treasonable. This seems to have worked for the time being, but it left an uncomfortable state of hostility. Richard at that time evidently felt himself sufficiently strong to defy the previous rebels in the Lords, since he then recalled the judges from Ireland, to where the Merciless Parliament had banished them. There was, meanwhile, the continuing disapproval by several parties, but particularly Gloucester, of Richard's placatory foreign policy.

One of the probable reasons for Richard's new feeling of strength was in fact just this foreign involvement. For some time he had been seeking an interview with Charles VI, king of

France, and in 1396 he achieved a truce with France on a stronger basis than anyone could have anticipated – that of marriage. He acquired the hand of the French monarch's daughter, the child Isabelle, then aged seven. The truce itself gave welcome relief from the costs of the war. But more crucial was a term proposed in the marriage agreement, to the effect that the French would support the English king with military aid 'against any of his subjects', should he need such help. Though this was not carried through in the final agreement, the threat of it must have put Gloucester and his supporters in a distinctly uncomfortable position.

In February Gloucester and Arundel declined to attend the Council. Probably they had by then been given reason to suppose that the king distrusted them. There were suspicions of a plot, though whether one existed or not is still open to doubt. In any case the eruption of this state of tension into action seems most likely to be due to mutual fear.

Warwick was arrested at a feast, on 10 July. The next day the arrests of Gloucester and Arundel took place; the former was at once exiled to Calais, and subsequently mysteriously murdered, no doubt at the king's instructions. Evidently Richard felt that to bring his uncle to judicial trial would have been too risky an act of defiance. He had shown his strength before, and he still commanded some support. The Earl of Arundel, who at first took to the safety of his castle, then surrendered. In September the king brought his accusations against the three to Parliament – that they were guilty of a 'great number of extortions, oppressions, grievances etc. committed against the king and people, and for other offences against the king's majesty'.

By the time Parliament heard the charges Gloucester was already dead. He was, it seems, suffocated at Calais, when under the charge of the Earl of Nottingham, the same Thomas Mowbray whose position had so often been interestingly ambiguous. Mowbray, in apparent recognition of his complicity, was then made Duke of Norfolk. Warwick, who had confessed, was imprisoned. The Earl of Arundel was executed. The effect was that by September 1397 Richard had conclusively removed all traces of overt opposition.

That he had felt the need of such strenuous self-protection is demonstrated by his activities during that summer. In July his agents had been recruiting an army, in that area of Cheshire to which he so often turned for loyal support; 2,000 Cheshire archers were brought south to back up his action at the September Parliament, a show of strength which must have had much to do with the production of the verdicts. Richard appeared surrounded by a considerable personal bodyguard.

The Parliament of 1397–8 reversed the infringements on the royal prerogative brought about by the Merciless Parliament ten years earlier. Ironically Richard used the same form of appeal against the three leaders of the Appellants as they themselves had used against his men. Richard then reinforced his loyal faction by distributing titles and lands, including five new dukedoms, and created John of Gaunt's son, by his mistress Katherine Swynford, Marquess of Dorset. Gaunt himself, once more returned, presided at the trials, and proved himself staunchly on the side of the throne. Richard consolidated his support in the north-west by annexing Arundel's Shropshire lands to Chester, and he filled with loyal supporters the castles of the marches and of North Wales. The situation was one of readiness and determination, rather than the ease of security.

What is most significant in all this is that the two younger Appellants, Bolingbroke and Mowbray, now Dukes of Hereford and Norfolk, remained quite unpunished. Their help was more valuable than any retribution against them could have been, for the time being. But this, as we shall see, was again the game of timing.

6 Richard's

Personal Reign

THE STATESMANSHIP of Richard II is inevitably overshadowed by the troubles and dangers of his life, but if the latter were brought on him partly by history and partly by character, the former were all very much his own.

Richard's first concern, and perhaps his major contribution to his period, was peace with France. We know that in the long run this did not last – hence Agincourt, and the martyrdom of Joan of Arc – but we may wonder what the result would have been had Richard lived to consolidate his plans.

As a first step Gaunt was sent as ambassador to France to start negotiations, and arrived in Calais in March 1392. Things did not, however, go easily. The French demanded the return of Calais, which Edward III had won for England with such determination. They were not, however, to succeed in this ambition until the end of the reign of Mary Tudor. Calais had become, and remained, an important psychological token to the English people. Froissart records that when it was rumoured that a French count had arrived in England to discuss a way of giving Calais back to the French it led to immediate national unrest. 'No single question could have disturbed the English people more than this.'

Neither Richard nor Gaunt would therefore have been foolish enough to accept such terms, and the truce consequently did not at once develop into a peace. It was, however, scheduled to last for four years from 1394; and this gave time for Richard to undertake the crucial ploy of his second marriage.

In the meantime there was still discontent of various sorts at home. In the same year as Gaunt went to France, 1392, angry scenes developed in London when the city refused to supply funds in the form of a loan to the Exchequer. Richard, as so often, acted high-handedly and in evident temper. He deposed the Mayor and removed the liberties of the city. The Londoners were to pay dearly for their defiance. They were in the end forced to buy their pardon at the cost of £10,000, and suffered in addition a £3,000 fine. The real upshot of all this, however, was that Richard effectively lost the backing of the city, which he might at any time need. Once again an over-reaction to an inferred slight on the royal dignity had won him enemies.

He governed in this period with the help of a Council composed both of friends and ex-enemies, in that Gloucester

PREVIOUS PAGES An illustration from Froissart's *Chronicles* showing Richard greeting Isabelle, daughter of Charles VI. He was to marry her after the death of Anne of Bohemia, and in doing so he cemented a truce with France which was to last for nearly thirty years.

was once again included. No doubt Richard liked to have that particular uncle where he could see him, and we shall find him taking him, rather against the Duke's inclination, on the expedition to Ireland. Providing a steadying influence as Chancellor was William of Wykeham, the much respected founder both of Winchester College and of New College, Oxford. Also on the Council was John of Gaunt, and his support and friendship were further secured by the granting of permanent favour to the Lancastrian line: the County Palatine of Lancaster was made hereditary for Gaunt's male heirs. The significance of this is highlighted for us by later events. When Edward III made Gaunt's Duchy a County Palatine he made Gaunt virtually a king, with powers of justice and revenue in a large slice of the realm transferred from the Crown to him. By making this privilege permanent Richard now virtually divided England. It is the supreme irony of his reign that this gift should be both disastrous to the throne because the heir to it was Bolingbroke, and less disastrous than it might have been because it ultimately led to Bolingbroke's becoming king.

A series of uprisings in 1393 has caused some puzzlement to historians, in that they do not appear to be spontaneous expressions of peasant discontent, but rather to be engineered by one or two individuals. It is, as so often, the 'why', rather than the 'what' or 'how', that eludes us. The background situation of peace, and the (by now) long military tradition in the provinces, provided the inflammable material of an unemployed professional soldiery. It is possible, and attractive as an explanation, that Gloucester and Arundel were somehow behind the trouble, since the risings started in Chester, where Gloucester had been appointed Justice, and Arundel was at his castle at Holt nearby. Neither made any attempt to intervene, though both were fully capable of doing so. Add to this that a major target of abuse throughout the risings was John of Gaunt himself, and we may perhaps justifiably suspect an attempt to influence the balance of power in the Council by means of the voice of popular feeling. The Chester revolt became linked to similar events in Yorkshire.

Gaunt returned from France and was sent north in person to deal with the conflict. He seems to have adopted a wisely moderate approach. He travelled first to Yorkshire, then to his

BELOW An illustration from a manuscript of the late fifteenth century showing William of Wykeham surrounded by benefactors and worthies. His notable achievements were the foundation of both Winchester College (OPPOSITE ABOVE) and New College, Oxford (OPPOSITE BELOW).

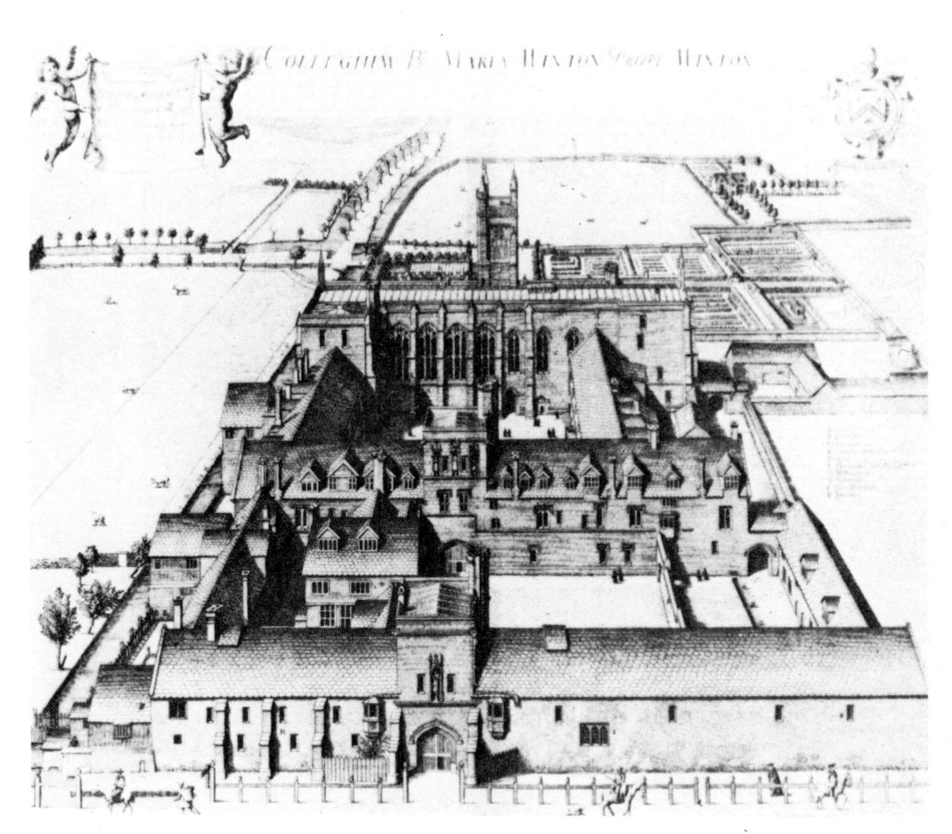

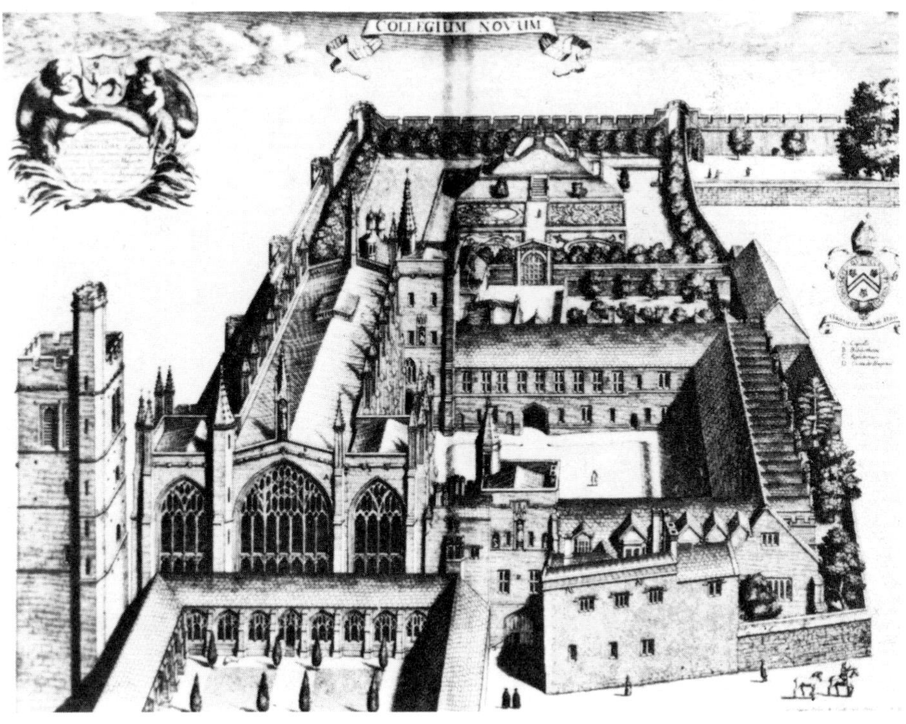
COLLEGIUM NOVUM

own County of Lancaster, and finally to Chester, and his presence, and no doubt that of his retainers, succeeded in restoring order. The following year, 1394, saw further attempts to blacken his character; but it seems that by now, at least in the north Midlands, he was not the object of real popular hatred. Arundel brought accusations against him at the spring Parliament of that year, but Parliament rejected them. Thomas Mowbray, Earl of Nottingham, was appointed Justice of Chester in place of Gloucester. The uprisings, in fact, were turned rather to Richard's advantage than against him.

In 1394 something of a turning-point in his life and career came about, symptomized by the death of his queen. Anne fell ill suddenly and died at the end of the first week of June, aged twenty-seven, at the palace of Sheen. We have seen that Richard reacted so passionately that he ordered the demolition of part of the palace. The funeral was held in Westminster Abbey, after a lying-in-state at St Paul's. Significantly the Earl of Arundel failed to attend the latter, was late arriving at the former, and fired Richard's touch-paper by asking to be excused from it early. His behaviour can hardly have been accidental, and his choice of the means of provocation of Richard, since such it must be, does no credit to his character. Richard hit him with a rod taken from a nearby verger, in the aisle of Westminster Abbey, drawing blood and knocking him to the ground, and we cannot help feeling that many less touchy people would have done the same. Arundel was arrested, but the king's temper cooled and he suffered only a week's imprisonment.

That was in June, and Richard set off for Wales en route to Ireland in August. Though some historians have seen this notable expedition as a reaction to bereavement, it cannot be so, since he was planning the large-scale exercise before Anne's unexpected death. He took Gloucester with him, leaving his uncle York as keeper of the realm; Gaunt went back to Aquitaine that same year, 1394. The royal Household moved slowly through Wales, in due course sailing from Haverfordwest, and reaching Ireland at Waterford on 2 October.

OPPOSITE The death of Richard's beloved queen Anne is shown here in an illustration from a copy of Froissart's *Chronicles*.

Henry II had set the pattern for the Irish policies and problems which were to bedevil subsequent medieval kings. His attempt at conquest and occupation in true Plantagenet fashion had been only partially successful. The principle was to

Richard's fleet leaving for Ireland. He sailed from Milford Haven to Waterford, from where the army marched to Dublin.

cordon off a large area around Dublin, known as the Pale (from the term for an enclosure), which was to be occupied for England by a martial barony. Beyond the Pale the Irish nobility retained their lands. Inevitably there was constant border conflict between the two groups, but by the time of Richard's reign the remaining occupying barons had started, in some cases, to go native. The deterioration of the administration was one of the causes of Richard's decision to intervene.

Ireland was in theory administered as if it were one of the Counties Palatine, and in theory it provided a revenue from land. The income, however, had dwindled, the costs of the administration had gone up, and in terms of Richard's economy it was now a drain rather than an asset. The negative and positive aspects of any reversal of this situation may have tempted him: to reduce an expense, and to gain, he hoped, a new source of income. A number of motives have been suggested, the simplest being the one he himself gave, that of reimposing law and order and bringing Ireland back under his own rule. The hope of peace with France, and hence also with Scotland, gave the opportunity. In view of the risings of 1393 it may also have been at the back of his mind that there existed an under-exercised soldiery in England, in need of engagement in some sort of military activity.

The royal army marched from Waterford to Dublin, and although there were no pitched battles they had continual skirmishing on the way. The Irish favoured guerrilla warfare, a form well suited to the wooded Leinster mountains. Froissart records a first-hand account which he heard at the English court: '. . . unless they choose, there is no one there to fight.' His informant paints a plainly biased picture of the Irish mentality, in which we can perhaps see the origins of a long-lived stereotype. They are hard to get to know, slow-thinking, uncouth, rough in their ways. It is even suggested at one point that they are cannibalistic: they remove the heart of a slain victim, and those who know their ways 'say that they eat it with great relish'. Clearly a bad press set in early.

Richard's army was well paid – it was funded by the merchants of the English cities – and displayed good order and effective strength. It was a combination of this show of might with careful diplomacy that enabled Richard to negotiate successfully with the Irish kings. He also brought into play the powerful argument of a naval blockade, which prevented any goods from entering or leaving the county – an indication that the Irish were not as primitive as Froissart's informant would have us believe, since they were evidently trading.

Richard succeeded in getting the four Irish kings to meet him in Dublin, though the discussions were hampered by a culture gap and by a language problem. Through interpreters he flattered them by offering them English knighthoods, although at first they failed to grasp the value of these, thinking that they already had honour enough. By such moderate means, and no doubt by the more forceful implications of what he could do if this failed, he got the desired homage from the Irish kings, who accepted him as Lord of Ireland. This was a personal title which may have added some security to his regal esteem, though it is doubtful if it meant much in practical terms. As Froissart's reporter put it: 'There is much honour in it, but the gain is small.'

There is much honour in it, but the gain is small.

The offer of knighthood carried with it the requirement of anglicization. It is amusing to notice already the characteristically English assumption that all people of different cultures are in need of being taught the proper way to behave. The kings were considered uncouth precisely because they used Irish customs, rather than respectable English ones. With true missionary zeal Richard set about having them taught proper table manners and a decent sense of social distinction, habits which, in accordance with their tradition, they quite lacked. Again as has so often happened, the Irish kings meekly accepted the correction, soon overcoming their doubts as to whether the new forms of behaviour were any better than their own, admitted themselves in error for not being respectably English, and lapped up their lessons in etiquette and social forms.

The parallel with later examples of our imperialist influence extends even to the matter of dress. Froissart's friend, who was entrusted by Richard with this job of socialization because he spoke the language, reports that the kings did not wear trousers – though the kilts they did wear must have seemed eminently sensible in comparison with the skin-tight hose of Richard's

The Irish kings were considered uncouth and barbarous by Richard's refined court. Richard attempted to civilize them and persuade them to adopt acceptable English conventions. Possibly this view of a king in a bath tub shows the first stage in the process.

court. He had a lot of linen drawers made, and, he says, 'I taught them to wear them and during the time I spent with them I cured them of many boorish and unseemly habits, both in dress and other matters.'

The king knighted them himself in the cathedral at Dublin, after an all-night vigil, and they sat at his table for the feast afterwards. Even in their new robes they looked strange and foreign, and everyone stared at them, somewhat spoiling their claim to the prerogative of good manners. If Richard's courtiers were wearing their little bowler hats at the time, the kings might well have stared back in equal amazement.

The English courtiers mocked the Irish kings for wearing kilts, and found them savage-looking even when they had been persuaded to wear trousers. The kings might well have stared with equal amazement at some of Richard's courtiers.

This interlude, so expressive of the medieval acceptance of the priority of ritual, was the outward façade of a sound political understanding. We are lucky enough to have Richard's own analysis of the Irish question, in a letter to York and the Council written in the spring of 1393, in which he identifies three groups of people as constituting the Irish population, one of which – the Anglo-Irish who had become in effect rebel colonists – posed a problem which demanded attention. He saw that this problem would be aggravated rather than solved by any high-handed action, and concluded that the solution was to consolidate the Pale by the introduction of more colonists:

> Because that in our land of Ireland there are three kinds of people, the Wild Irish our enemies, the Irish Rebels, and the obedient English, it appeared to us and our council that, considering that the Irish rebels are perhaps so rebellious by reason of the grievances and wrongs done unto them on the one part, and that redress hath not been made to them on the other part; and that likewise if they be not wisely managed, and put into good hope of favour, they will probably join our enemies; wherefore, it shall not be any fault of ours that a general pardon be granted them.

As a cogent assessment followed by a coherent plan it is the work of a statesman; in its slightly devious gambit of turning potential enemies into friends by harmless placation it is very much Richard's.

Early in 1395 the Council in London sent a message to Richard asking him to return. Evidently he was not ready to do so, since he lingered in Ireland overseeing his programme, and a personal delegation by the Archbishop of York and the Bishop of London was necessary to persuade him. The first letter had referred to trouble impending from the Scots, and 'other important reasons which would be explained more fully to the king on his return'. It was perhaps these reasons which the bishops explained in person to Richard in Dublin.

We should, of course, dearly like to know what they were. The probability seems to be that the Council was worried by the stirrings of the Lollard Movement, which came to a head in 1395. Perhaps it would have been rash to express doubt about the Lollards in a letter, since they had many sympathizers at high level. The fact that it was two prominent bishops who eventually went to Richard indicates that this guess may be correct, since Lollardy was primarily an anti-clerical movement, and its main threat was to the established Church. Their arguments, whatever they were, were convincing: Richard returned in May, leaving the Earl of March, his heir presumptive, as his personal lieutenant.

The origin of the word 'lollard' has caused some speculation. In fact it comes from the Middle Dutch word *lollen*, meaning to mumble, and the noun 'lollaerd' was applied to those who muttered or mumbled their prayers. It was used abusively of the Flemish heretics, and seems to have been transferred from there to England by the year 1382, when it was used in an anti-Wyclif sermon. Lollards were at first simply the followers of Wyclif, though as these became more diffused and less clearly committed to Wyclif's teaching it might be truer to say that Lollards were also those who could be confused with the followers of Wyclif. At any rate the term was used only by their enemies.

John Wyclif, who died in 1384, was a religious reformer who to a surprising extent anticipated the Reformation, and indeed the non-conformist movement. His message was that both clergy and laymen should follow the 'meek and poor and charitable life of Christ'. He preached a form of individualism, each man's soul being the seat of his religion. A direct relationship between man and God was thus possible, and the effect of this was to diminish seriously the role of the priest as intercessor. Wyclifite teaching also rejected the miracle of transubstantiation, and initiated the idea of consubstantiation – a technical point of sacramental religion which was to have much importance for Anglicanism. Briefly, they believed that the bread and wine of the Eucharist remained bread and wine, rather than actually changing into the body and blood of Christ, but that they contained within them the body and blood of Christ in mystical form.

Wyclif, who taught at Oxford, caught the attention of both high and low. His anti-clericalism had a wide appeal. The belief that the Church should not hold material wealth led to the suggestion that it should be disendowed, a promising source of funds which was later to be put into practice, though only against a section of the Church, by Henry VIII. It was perhaps this aspect which appealed to John of Gaunt, who saw the possibility of raising funds by such means for the French wars. He, at any rate, acted as Wyclif's patron, as indeed he did as Chaucer's, and a more unlikely combination of plutocrat and reformer is hard to imagine. The king's mother, Princess Joan, also favoured Wyclif, protecting him on one occasion against proceedings instigated by the Pope.

In 1382 he achieved official recognition in the form of a ban prohibiting him from teaching, but no doubt foreseeing this he had already left Oxford in 1381 and retired to his rectory at Lutterworth, where he was to spend the remainder of his life turning out pamphlets and organizing a band of disciples. He wrote now in English (previously in Latin), and his tracts began to gain popular, rather than scholarly, support. Together with a number of Oxford scholars he also undertook a comprehensive translation of the Bible into the vernacular, which had previously only been partially attempted.

One might say that about this time Wyclifism became Lollardy. We read in the Statutes of the Realm for 1381–2: 'There be divers evil persons within the realm, going from county to county, and from town to town, in certain habits under dissimulation of great holiness and without the license of the ordinaries of the places or other sufficient authority, preaching daily, not only in churches and churchyards but also in markets, fairs, and other open places, where a great congregation of people is, divers sermons containing heresies and notorious errors.' Thus it is clear that a popular movement was in progress by the early 1380s. Wyclif's original band of missionaries, with their stimulating brand of anti-clerical

Bi ye boke leuyner of prinues

Blisful ye man yt wente [in the title: of prophete dd of]
not awei i ye counseil of vn
pitouse & i ye weie of synful stod not:
& i ye chayer of pestilence sat not. But i
ye lawe of ye lord his wil & i ye lawe of hy
he shal sweteli thenken day & nyȝt. And
he shal be as a tree yt is plauntid besides ye
doun rennyngis of watris: yt his frute shal
ȝyue i his tyme. And ye lef of hy shal not
fallen & alle thingis whit euer he shal don
shuln maken welsu. Not so ye vnpitouse
not so: but as poudre yt ye wynd throwith fro ye
face of ye erye. Yerfore eft
risen not ye vnpitouse i dom: ne synful
i ye counseil of riȝtwise. For ye lord hath
knowe ye weie of ye riȝtwise: & ye goynge
of ye vnpitouse shal perschen. ye psalm of dauy

Why gnastiden gentilis: & puplis
thoȝten veyn thingis.
Yer stoden nee ye kyngis of ye erye:
& princis camen togide i to oon aȝen ye lord &
aȝen his crist. Go breke wee ye bondis of
he: & aferr throwe wee fro vs ye ȝok of he.
Yat dwellith i heuenes shal scorne he
& ye lord shal bemowe he. Yanne he
shal speke to ye i his wrathe: & i his wood
nesse disturben ye togide. I forsoye am
sett kyng fro hy vp on Syon ye holy mount
of hym prechinge his heste. Ye lord seide to me
my sone yu art: i today gat yee. Aske of
me & i shal ȝyue to yee gentilis yyn eritage
& yi possessioun ye tmes of ye erye. Yow shalt
gouerne ye i an yrene ȝerde: & as a vessel
of a crockere breke ye togide. And now
kyngis vnderstondith: beth taȝt yat demen ye
erye. Serueth to ye lord i drede: & ful out
gladeth to hy wt tremblinge. Takith disciplyne
ne lest any tyme be wraththed ye lord: & ȝee
perische fro ye riȝtwis weye. Whan his wraththe
shal brennen out i short: blisful alle yat
trosten in hym. psalm to dd whanne he fliȝde

Lord whi be multiplied yt trublen me: manye
aȝen me. Manye seyn to my soule: yer is
not helthe to hy i his god. Yow forsoye lord
art myn vndertaker: my glorie & en
haunsinge myn heued. With my vois to
ye lord i cride: & he ful out herde me fro his
holy hil. I slepte & was aslepe & full out

ros: for ye lord vndertoke me. I shal not
drede thousendis of puple goynge aboute
me: rise vp lord make me saf my god.
For yu hast smyten alle doynge aduersite
to me wiyoute cause: ye teey of ye synful
yu hast tobrosid. Of ye lord is helye & vp on
yi puple yi blessynge. In to ye ende i dities
ye psalm of dd or i to ye ende ye psalm of ye sons of dauy.

When i inwardly clepede ful out
herde me ye god of my riȝtwisnesse
i tribulacioun yu spraddist out to me. Haue
mercy of me & ful out here myn orisoun. Sones of men hou longe wt greuous herte:
wherto loue ȝee vanyte
& sechen lesyng. And witey for ye lord
hay maad merueilous his seint: ye lord
ful out shal heere me whan i shal crien to
hym. Wraththe ȝee & willey not synne: yat
ȝee seyn i ȝoure hertis & i ȝoure couchis
haue ȝee compunccioun. Sacrifisey sacrifise
of riȝtwisnesse & hopey i ye lord: manye
seyn who shewith to vs gode thingis. Mer
kid is vp on vs ye liȝt of yi chere lord:
yu ȝeue gladnesse i myn herte. Of ye
frute of whete wyn & oile of he: yei
ben multiplied. In pes i to itself: i shal
slepe & resten. For yu lord: singulerly
i hope hast togidere set me. In to ye ende for hir yat
getiy ye eritage.

My wordis wt eris par
ceyue yu lord: vnder
stond my cry. Tak heede to ye vois
of myn orisoun: my kyng & my god. For
to yee i shal preyen lord: erly yu ful out
shalt here my vois. Erly i shal neeȝ
stonde to yee & seen: for yu art god not
willinge wickednesse. Ne shal dwelle
beside yee ye shrewe: ne shul dwellen
stille ye vnriȝtwise before yyn eȝen. You
hast hatid alle yt werke wickednesse:
yu shalt leesen alle yt speke lesyng. Ye
man of bloodis & trecherous ye lord shal
wlate: i forsoye i ye multitude of yi mercy.
I shal entren i to yyn hous: i shal honou
re at yyn holi temple i yi drede. Lord bring
forth me i yi riȝtwisnesse for myn ene
mys: mak redi i yi siȝte my weie. For
yer is not i ye mouy of he treuye: ye herte
of he is veyn. An open sepulcre is ye
yrote of he: wt her tungis trecherousli
yei diden: deme he yu god. Falle yei
doun fro her youȝtis: after ye multitude of
ye vnpitousnessis of he put hem awey.

revivalism based on poverty and on scriptural study, must quickly have attracted imitators and the sort of fringe element which always gets drawn to such movements. A more fanatical attitude became characteristic of this second-phase movement. But the combination of an emphasis on poverty with an attack on the rich clergy was a formula for success in the late fourteenth century. To the world inhabited by Langland's Piers Plowman, and to the people in the inn visited by Chaucer's Canterbury pilgrims, it much have had the attraction of relevance. What is slightly more surprising is that it also appealed to the nobility. This fact, supported by the literature of the court as well as the country, brings home to us the extent to which the Church had become a national issue.

Lollardy also made use of the new fashion for Englishness, in that (like the literary movement after Chaucer) it made the English language its special medium. The preachers used the common tongue and referred to the English Bible. In this too they united the tastes both of court and country people, and if their attack on ostentation and adornment may have rankled slightly at Eltham or Sheen, at least their other notable feature, their rigid pacificism, would have harmonized at the time with some aspects of official policy.

Richard himself remained orthodox but tolerant. However, the mission of the two bishops, as messengers from the Council, to recall him from Ireland indicates some possible disquiet in those around him. There is no doubt that already Lollardy had some support in the court, and in Richard's absence its influence may have been spreading in the Council itself. A detailed petition was presented to Parliament in 1395 setting out the main tenets of Lollardy. The statement was also nailed to the doors of St Paul's Cathedral for popular attention. It accused the Church of being dominated by temporal possessions, having no support in scripture, of idolatry on the one hand and secularism on the other. With far-sighted courage it opposed priestly chastity and the rite of confession. After the Reformation we can hardly find these things shocking, but it must have been clear at the time that the reformers had gone too far. They had embarked on heresy.

Richard's return was effective. Those who had been Lollard supporters in his absence at once became good orthodox

OPPOSITE A page from the earliest surviving Wyclif Bible, of the late fourteenth century.

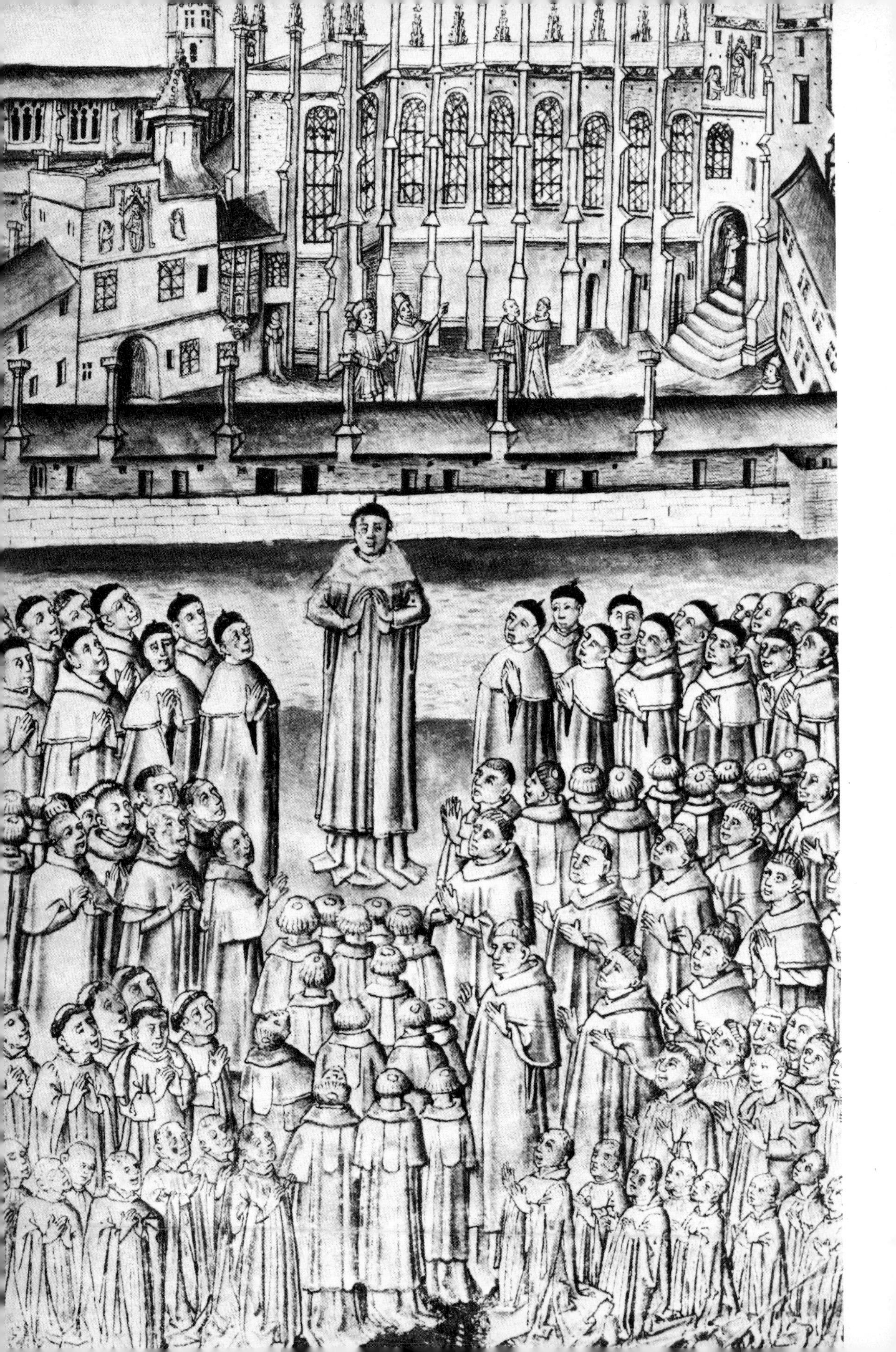

Christians. Lollardy became invisible. Clearly its adherents were too cautious or too wise to risk the martyrdom of heretics, and for some time the whole movement went underground. In that state it could incubate all the more effectively, and in due course it returned in resurrected forms. Wyclif was the spiritual ancestor not only of Luther but also of Wesley.

Richard's thoughts were now turning towards his revenge for the humiliations brought on him by the Appellants. Confident from his success in Dublin, and more in command of circumstances than ever before, he risked, in a typically personal form, a grand gesture of defiance. Robert de Vere had been hated by the Lords Appellant as strongly as he had been loved by Richard, and indeed largely for that reason. In 1392 he had died in exile, as a result of an accident at a boar hunt near Louvain. On his return from Ireland Richard had the body brought back for reburial at Earls Colne, the site of the de Vere family vault in Essex. He organized an expensive and elaborate

OPPOSITE New College Oxford, not long after its foundation, showing the strong ecclesiastical nature of education at the time when Wyclif was teaching.

ABOVE Monks were among the privileged few who were able to study academically. This illustration from a manuscript belonging to Sidney Sussex College, Cambridge, shows different orders at work.

ceremony, and undertook a gesture of personal commitment and defiance which, in its dramatic emotionalism, is strongly characteristic. He had the coffin opened, wishing to see his friend's face again. De Vere's corpse had been embalmed, evidently fairly effectively; Richard placed a ring on his finger. The nobles had mostly stayed away from the ceremony – Gloucester, Arundel, Warwick and Derby were all absent. Though they were spared direct confrontation with this sign that Richard had not forgotten, no doubt the message went fast enough to those for whom it was probably intended.

During these few years Richard was consistently proving that he was nobody's puppet, not even history's. In view of the long background of the war it could hardly have been expected that he would be so successful in his personal quest for peace.

Richard was aged twenty-nine and, Froissart reports, looking around for a suitable new bride. The only dynastic alliance available was with the daughter of the king of France, and it is significant that Richard was now so able to ignore or defy public opinion as to press for this. One of his informants told Froissart on his visit to Eltham that the intention 'has caused some dismay in this country, that he should marry his adversary's daughter. It does him no good with his people, but he takes no notice.' Such was the talk at court in 1395.

In France in the meantime the request was received with surprise verging on incredulity. Richard's ambassadors were well received; but some of Charles's advisers felt that a securer peace should be settled first. France and England were still technically enemies. Others however saw the advantage of encouraging by this means a more lasting peace.

Isabelle was aged six at the beginning of the negotiations, seven on her marriage. By all accounts she was precocious and self-confident. She evidently liked the idea (what six-year-old girl would not?) of being queen of England, 'for they tell me I should then be a great lady'. She had been trained to royalty and, we are told, knew well how to behave like a queen.

Gloucester, of course, was bitterly opposed; the Duke of York vacillated; but Gaunt was in favour, and that counted for much. His own two daughters had become queens of Castile and of Portugal, a sure sign of his appreciation of the diplomatic possibilities of treaty by marriage. He was back in England at

The meeting of Richard and his child-bride Isabelle. She was only seven years of age when they married in March, 1396, but was far from daunted by the prospect of becoming queen of England.

the end of 1395, when he himself also undertook a rather surprising marriage, legitimizing his long-standing liason with Katherine Swynford, by whom he already had four children.

The temporary truce with France was extended to twenty-five years in December 1395, thus providing a more acceptable context for the marriage. It was extended again to twenty-eight years the next spring, and Richard was married by proxy to Isabelle in March. He went to France himself amid much pageantry, banqueting ceremonially with the French king. The child Isabelle made a state entry into London that November, and was crowned queen of England the following January, 1397.

The marriage and its long preliminaries had been expensive.

Premierement sist larcevesq
de Reins. Apres seoit
lempereur. Apres seoit
le Roy ainsi comme ou milieu
du front de la sale. Apres
le Roy de france seoit le roy

des romains. Et avoit autant de distance
du Roy au Roy des romains comme du
Roy a lempereur. Et avoient lempereur
le Roy et le Roy des romains chascun se-
pareement un ciel de drap dor borde de velu
au aus armes de france. et par dessus ceulx

At one point the English delegation negotiating in Paris was said to number 500. Richard, as had become his habit, spared no expense in the lavishness of ceremony and the generosity of gifts. It did, however, have the effect of saving further expense, for twenty-eight years, in warfare against the French. A more significant result for history is that it effectively ensured, by Isabelle's extreme youth, that Richard would have no heir.

It was recognized at the time that his successor would be Roger Mortimer, the Earl of March, who was the son of Philippa, the heiress of Edward III's second son Lionel, Duke of Clarence, who had died in 1368. March, however, was to die before the king, in 1398, thus leaving the throne in extreme vulnerability to dispute for the succession. In due course March's daughter, Anne Mortimer, was to marry Richard, Earl of Cambridge, the son of the Duke of York, thus uniting the lines of two of Edwards III's five sons. This became the Yorkist line, and a powerful contender against the Lancastrians for the legitimate entitlement to the throne.

Richard, however, was not yet dead, nor apparently at all aware of the gathering threats. No doubt he still thought he would live long enough for Isabelle to bear him an heir, and in the meantime March was popular and capable. We find signs during the 1390s of an unrealistic over-importance in Richard's view of himself. In 1397 he even used the title 'emperour', and his rash extravagance in granting pensions to Electors in Germany is some evidence that he had ambitions to the Imperial throne. His achievement of peace was a powerful basis for the extension of his influence. For the brief phase of a couple of years we have a glimpse into another possible world, from one of those rare watersheds when the history of England and of Europe was poised to take a totally different course to the one which in the end formed reality. What-might-have-been has its own special nostalgia. But once again Richard's personal qualities intrude, and take history by surprise.

LEFT A ceremonial banquet at the French court, such as Richard attended in celebration of his marriage.

7 The Fal

# of a King

HENRY BOLINGBROKE has already appeared many times in this story. Even during Richard's fairly short reign he had an active and wide-ranging career. Born in 1367, he was the same age as the king. Like that of his father, and following the custom of the time, his name 'of Bolingbroke' was taken from the place where he happened to have been born. Bolingbroke is a village in Lincolnshire, not far from the Wash.

Apart from the involvement in Richard's affairs which we have from time to time noted, Henry had adventures of his own, cramming what must seem to us a lot of life into a few years. After Richard's resumption of personal power at the end of the Appellants' revolt Bolingbroke set off to Prussia on a crusade, from which he had returned, wreathed in glory and fame, in time to join Gaunt's peace mission to France in 1392. Two years later, when Richard marched to Dublin, he was away again on a pilgrimage to the Holy Land. He was back home and present with the other Lords Appellant when in 1397 Richard, suspecting them of hatching or being about to hatch a plot, ordered the arrest of Warwick and Arundel.

From Richard's earliest youth his cousin and contemporary had been a familiar figure. Indeed he played a part in the young king's coronation. The two, however, were very different both in appearance and in attitude. It would be wrong to present Henry Bolingbroke as a man of action purely, since he had the same artistic and literary tastes as Richard, perpetuating on his accession the high cultural standards of the court, and since he also inherited at least a part of his father's knack for diplomacy. But he was in his youth an athlete, a successful jouster, and he lacked Richard's elegance. He was stockily, sturdily built.

Bolingbroke was from the start in an ambiguous position. He had his father's vast Lancastrian interests behind him, and for much of the time the Duchy of Lancaster was firmly committed to supporting the king. Yet he sided at the crucial moment with the Gloucester faction, an act which alienated him, permanently as it turned out, from Richard's trust. Yet at the same time he was set apart from the Appellants, since his existence itself formed a barrier to any ambition Gloucester might have had. And for most of the time he was actively disputing with Gloucester over the Bohun inheritance, which was to be divided between them, the method of division being the subject

PREVIOUS PAGE Henry Bolingbroke, shown here wearing a tall black hat, claims the throne of England.

This early effigy of Henry IV is in the shrine of Charlemagne at Aachen Cathedral.

of long-drawn-out disagreement. Anybody who could keep afloat in such cross-currents would need to be capable and ingenious.

Mary Bohun, whom he married through his father's cunning arrangements, produced for him a son, born in the castle at Monmouth, a property of the Duchy of Lancaster, in 1387. No one could have foreseen that this would be the great Henry V, the victor of Agincourt. Mary died in 1394, the same year as Richard's Anne and as John of Gaunt's second wife Constanza.

As so often, one can point to the causes of what took place only with the advantage of hindsight. They simply could not have guessed, in 1397, what the ultimate outcome of Richard's treatment of the Appellants would be. The situation was that Mowbray and Bolingbroke, now the Dukes of Norfolk and Hereford, were in an apparently secure position. Richard needed their help and support, and had exempted them from the punishments rained on the other Appellants. The Duke of

Hereford in particular, with his powerful weapon of the balancing effect of the Lancastrian inheritance, must have seemed set for a career of peaceful power. There is no sign that he was unduly ambitious. He had, and could expect to receive, all he could want.

The roots of what went wrong are deep, and little of them is apparent on the surface. The sudden flurry of action was sparked off by dramatic and clearly visible events which it would be easy to mistake for causes. They were rather the first part of the effects.

A truly feudal monarchy might have started with some realistic basis of support, being a land-holding barony on a large scale, and having the moral, legal and traditional right to demand support from fiefholders in exchange for wielding its power to protect the status quo. In England evidently things could not remain so simple, and from a very early stage our monarchy had started to become constitutional. The king had gradually lost any understood natural right to revenue: he had to find means of acquiring it. This exercise might take several forms, but since money could be got only from those who had it, it soon became apparent that the best means of extracting it from them was by their consent. This requirement, which quickly became the formula of the consent of Parliament, might always be withheld, and was granted conditionally on the understanding that the revenue was put to approved use. The arrangement had in fact already become contractual. Thus, underlying monarchy in England in the Middle Ages (and thereafter) was an inherent paradox. The king must have funds in order to remain powerful. But he could get funds only by relegating a portion of his power.

Richard II ran an increasingly costly court. The running expenses of his Household alone are estimated to have been, in present-day terms, close on £1,000,000 a year. He was profusely, almost manically, generous. The distribution of pensions in France and Germany may have had sound political ends, but even if so they were ends which a more cautious head of state might have considered to be beyond his country's means. The shower of grants and gifts which accompanied his second marriage is in keeping with the expenses of the undertaking itself. One account estimates that it cost £200,000,

ABOVE AND BELOW
Hunting scenes from medieval manuscripts. The sport of kings, hunting was no doubt one of the costly indulgences of Richard's court that contributed to his financial problems.

and a translation into modern terms makes that an incredible £6,000,000.

In 1397 royal finances were in such poor shape that Richard, casting around for new means of raising revenue, resorted to what amounted to a system of forced loans. The rich were obliged to make loans to the state, in exchange for letters patent guaranteeing repayment. Probably scepticism about Richard's integrity took the edge off the apparent respectability of these, and one of the major effects was the alienation of the burgesses and corporations who were obliged to provide. The idea might have worked well enough – at least it brought in a much-needed £20,000 – but Richard made the mistake of going too far. The citizens of London and of some of the more influential towns began to regard him as a danger.

His next step took him a good deal further into the dangerous area of popular distrust, though even this was not to be his most disastrous. The Parliament which sat at the end of 1397 had taken the crucial step of declaring the rising of 1387 treasonable. The king, whose mind was evidently on money, saw a fruitful chance offered by this move. He imposed a set of fines intended to recover the royal pleasure, known as *La Plesaunce*. Those shires which were said to have supported the rebels were deemed liable to this fine, the burden falling most heavily on London and the south-east. Significantly he exempted the territory of the north-west Midlands, to which he had always turned for friendly support. So remote was the extortion from its supposed cause that it seemed to all rich owners of land or town property that any means might now be taken to deprive them of their wealth. Richard's next set of actions, motivated by the same financial insecurity, was the most reckless of his life, and is even seen by some as indicating the onset of mental instability.

John of Gaunt died in February 1399. He had reached what was then the grand age of fifty-nine, and it seems likely that a decline in his health during the previous year may account for the rather surprising events of the early part of it.

The 1397 Parliament had reassembled at Shrewsbury in January 1398, and its amenability from then on may partly be explained by its location, in territory friendly to Richard. No doubt he was supported by his Cheshire archers. Even so he revealed a sense of insecurity by insisting on the renewal of oaths of allegiance, including in these even his likely heir the Earl of March, summoned by a flying visit from his post in Dublin. March, however, was to be murdered by Irish rebels later that year. In the meantime Richard had held for himself a sinister safeguard. Parliament had permitted the pardoning of the 1387 traitors in exchange for the penalties of *La Plesaunce*; but it also agreed to Richard's maintaining a list of fifty unnamed exceptions to the pardon. That they were unnamed perhaps meant that the list was mutable, and hence that a large number of people might feel themselves at risk of imminent arrest and execution for as long as the exceptions remained unnamed. It was at this Shrewsbury Parliament, and most probably as a result of the secret exceptions to the pardons, that the quarrel of Bolingbroke and Thomas Mowbray became public.

It was a quarrel which, whatever its causes, was to have crucial historical effects. Both the younger Appellants must have known their danger throughout the period following their revolt, and Richard's latest step merely seemed to indicate that their fate was closing in on them. We can guess that what actually happened sprang in some way from this situation. What was said to have happened bears some credibility.

Bolingbroke told Richard of a conversation between him and Mowbray. They had been on the road together, riding to London, the previous month. Mowbray had asked him whether he knew that they were in danger. Bolingbroke (so he said) professed ignorance, and Mowbray further spoke of a plot to remove both him and his father, Gaunt. He suggested counter-action before it was too late. Bolingbroke, so he claimed, was shocked, and refused to get involved. Instead he brought the story to the king.

It was a difficult and an interesting situation for Richard, and the course of events shows that he saw it primarily as the chance he had been waiting for to dispose of the two remaining Appellants. As usual his first reaction was to play for time. He first had the charge repeated by Bolingbroke to Parliament, thus both demonstrating its genuineness and making it sufficiently public not to be ignored. Then he dissolved Parliament.

Business was to be completed by a parliamentary committee, a normal procedure but in this case a device which allowed Richard more control. The committee consisted of knights and lords, and included some of the most powerful magnates – the Dukes of Lancaster and York and the Earls of March and Northumberland. Richard's close supporters were also represented, such as the chamber-knights Bushy and Green, who turn up as his servants in Shakespeare's play.

The committee met in March at Bristol, and Bolingbroke, appearing before it, added some new charges against Mowbray. He was now accused, among other things, of having arranged the death of Gloucester, uncle both to the accuser and to the king. Though it might have been convenient for Richard to get the blame for this clearly apportioned, there seems to have been no undue influence on the committee. In due course it decided that Bolingbroke had not produced sufficient evidence to prove his case, which it was therefore unable itself to decide. In accordance with medieval custom the matter was referred to the Court of Chivalry, that is, to trial by combat.

This means of deciding an issue was, we must understand, regarded as every bit as certain a proof of innocence or guilt as trial by argument is today. Yet already we have seen signs that it must have started to appear anachronistic, since the fate of several accused men in this story was decided by lengthy and meticulous legal proceedings. Both the ex-mayor Brembre accused by the Appellants, and the Appellant Arundel accused by Richard's supporters, had asked for trial by combat – but both had been refused it. Taking the matter to Chivalry now must have seemed like a reversion to a past age.

The event was fixed to take place at Coventry that September. The further delay gave Richard the chance to consider how to make the most of it. On the face of it there was considerable danger for him. According to Froissart his advisers warned him to remain uninvolved. Bolingbroke was highly popular, particularly in London. Yet Richard must have pondered the possible outcome, which would have had its bitter effects for him whichever one of the combatants won. If Bolingbroke won, his popularity, particularly among those now less favourable to Richard, would entrench him in a position which would threaten to rival the throne. If he lost,

OPPOSITE A jousting scene from a British Museum manuscript, with ladies of the court looking on. The Court of Chivalry must have presented a similarly magnificent spectacle.

Though the duel between Henry Bolingbroke and Thomas Mowbray was to be an affair of international importance, it was nevertheless something of a return to a past fashion. The custom of trial by single combat as a means of testing guilt had fallen out of use during Richard's reign.

Gaunt would never forgive the king for allowing it to happen. In either case there would still be one victorious ex-Appellant to be dealt with.

Preparations for the encounter were ostentatious, and tinged with the glory of romance. It was to be a truly European affair, in the grand medieval style which had been rather subdued during those years. A duel to the death between two such famous and important knights (one, after all, the cousin of the king, the other the Earl Marshal of England) naturally produced the sort of anticipation which occurs only rarely in any age. The Duke of Milan sent armourers from Lombardy to fit Bolingbroke out with suitably sumptuous gear, and Mowbray sent for equipment from Germany. Tourists began to arrive in Britain for the event. It was clearly to be a fashionable society occasion.

In view of all this – the public interest and the public nature of the exercise – it must have taken courage or the determination of a trapped man for Richard to step in and spoil the fun. He waited until the very last minute before doing so, perhaps with his own sense of drama, perhaps because still genuinely undecided. The tension and the shock of the decision are well caught in the third scene of Shakespeare's play, which described events much as the chroniclers indicated them to have been.

Bolingbroke, on a white horse, came into the lists first. The king mounted his throne with all the peers of the realm in accompaniment. Mowbray entered, and the fanfare proclaimed the start of the joust. Then the king stood and threw down his staff.

Two hours of discussion apparently followed, during which the duellists and the public were kept in suspense and ignorance. No doubt the main debate was between Richard and his uncle Gaunt, since the latter's agreement was essential to any sort of solution. Bushy, acting as secretary to the king, eventually read out a lengthy document. It gave the king's judgement: in terms of the Court of Chivalry Richard was within his rights in personally intervening to stop the fight. The taking of this opportunity enabled him to distribute sentences which a legal court had hesitated to commit itself to.

Bolingbroke was to be exiled for ten years. On a plea from Gaunt Richard reduced this to six. Mowbray's exile, however,

A miniature in a manuscript illumination shows Richard conferring with Thomas Mowbray.

in recognition that he was the guilty party, was to be for life. But if his guilt was acknowledged, then why was Bolingbroke sentenced at all? The motivations of the dramatic event are easier to follow than its logic. Froissart tells us that the lords who were present received the announcement with satisfaction, but presumably they had already been consulted. Above all we would like to know what was the state of Gaunt's health. There is something almost actuarial about the reduction of the ten years to six. In the event this proved to be more than a safe risk for Richard.

Mowbray set off at once for Holland, and embarked from there on a pilgrimage to Jerusalem. A year after his departure he died in Venice, broken in spirit by his exile and his fall from power. Bolingbroke made his way to France, sent off with memorable good will by the citizens of London, and took up residence at the court of the French king, where he possessed personal popularity and support. With friends both at home and abroad he could hardly have represented any less of a threat to Richard there, and only the lack of his ominous presence at the English court was gained. No doubt he was still on Richard's mind. He had gone, moreover, with the crucial promise that he would receive his inheritance without hindrance, whether still in exile or not. It must have seemed a powerful guarantee of his future power, at least if he had temporarily forgotten the ease with which Richard could reverse his promises.

That was in September 1398. On 3 February 1399 John of Gaunt died at his house in Holborn, presenting Richard with the most delicate situation of his reign. The most powerful citizen in his realm was in exile, ostensibly as a traitor, but with little moral and no legal justification for this verdict. The reduced sentence of exile threatened his fairly imminent return. If the events of the previous year are to be taken at their face value, Richard's dilemma was now acute. If, on the other hand, the sentence had itself been part of a plot, a careful gamble with time in Richard's true style, by which the slow fuse would in the inevitable course of events destroy the one remaining threat to the king's security, then the situation is even more interesting and no less dramatic. Either interpretation gives the same result: Richard was now in a position to acquire the vast Lancastrian wealth.

The solution to the threat left over from the revolt of the Appellants was also the solution to the main cause of his insecurity, his lack of funds. Richard's fear of Henry's power was undoubtedly real, being based on past experience. The great temptation of annexing the Lancastrian estates to the Crown would in any case have been almost irresistible. It presented the monarchy with the promise of permanent security. It is an added irony, in the light of history, that this result was to be achieved by Richard's successor, Henry Bolingbroke, and as a direct result of Richard's attempt to gain it now.

Richard on campaign in Ireland, bestows a knighthood on the future Henry v, the son of his enemy Henry Bolingbroke, who, unknown to the king, is planning to return to England and confront him.

Richard has some arguments in exoneration of a deed which has seemed to many (influenced by the succeeding events) to be the act of a tyrant. It is all too easy, but unfair to the participants, to read history backwards. The inheritance of someone exiled for treason would naturally be forfeited, and it would naturally fall to the Crown. To allow Henry to inherit would moreover jeopardize the peace of the realm, threatening (at best) the loss of power of the monarchy, which in the nation's interests the monarch has a duty to maintain, and (at worst) the eruption of civil war. Richard did not act in haste or with any sign of personal arbitrariness. In accordance with much of the doings of his reign he sought legal means. He first recalled the Parliamentary committee.

The lawyers consulted found that the grant of power to inherit in exile had been incompatible with the sentence of exile for treason. As might have been expected, they found it right that a traitor's inheritance should pass to the Crown. Though it is by no means clear how Bolingbroke had proved himself a traitor, that was his status in the eyes of the king and the committee. The conclusion has rather the appearance of inverted reasoning: he had been sentenced to exile, therefore he was a traitor. But possibly Richard had now decided to play the Joker he had dealt himself at the Shrewsbury Parliament, the flexible variable of the unnamed exceptions to the pardon for the earlier revolt.

Bolingbroke's exile was at once extended for life. The letters of attorney which had empowered him to inherit when he was deported were revoked. By these acts his property was in effect confiscated on 18 March 1399, although the official announcement of the confiscation and the life-exile was not made until May, by which time Richard was on his way to Ireland.

This too was no sudden or impetuous decision, odd though it may seem to us in the light of subsequent events. He had been raising an army for the expedition all spring. An immediate, and probably sufficient, cause for this had been the murder late the previous year of his personal representative there, the Earl of March.

Richard sailed from Milford Haven to Waterford, as before, arriving on 1 June. He took with him a large court, which included the young son of Henry Bolingbroke, the future

Henry V. Richard knighted him in Ireland, further adding to the situation's irony. The Percys – the Earl of Northumberland and his son – had been expected to attend the expedition, but significantly they evaded it. Richard left at home the weak-willed Duke of York as Keeper of the Realm. It was perhaps not to his advantage that most of the loyal magnates were with him in Ireland.

Clearly he saw the trip as part of a continuing policy, the assertion and restoration of his royal power. Had he not gone the colony of Ireland would have been lost to England, perhaps for ever. But his leaving the country shows him to have been quite unaware of the extent of his danger. This is not surprising. Negotiations and communications with the French court had remained friendly, and Richard had every reason to suppose that Henry would stay obediently, and comfortably, in exile.

Circumstances in Paris were, however, changing; rivalry between the Dukes of Burgundy and Orleans had created a climate in which the reopening of Anglo-French hostility would help the latter's faction, and it was probably with the help of Orleans that Henry began to muster arms. He had in the meantime been joined in Paris by supporters such as the young Thomas Fitzalan and the ex-Archbishop Arundel.

Richard marched to Dublin, not without some difficulties on the way. His problem was, as before, finding the enemy. The king of Leinster refused to negotiate, and Richard was waiting in Dublin while his troops searched for the king in the mountains, when Sir William Bagot, his friend and the leader of the chamber-knights, brought the news. Bad weather had cut Ireland off for several days, and it was not until about 10 July that Richard heard what had happened.

Bolingbroke had left Paris for Brittany, but probably changed course for the Channel and seized three ships at Boulogne, from where he crossed to Britain. He put in at Pevensey, perhaps for supplies, then sailed north. His final landing was at Ravenspur, on the Humber, which he reached on about 4 July. It was conveniently close to a number of his castles, and to the territory of his likely supporters, the Percys.

Henry at once set about raising support in Yorkshire. Lancastrian knights flocked to him. Word spread fast, and he was soon surrounded by more supporters than he could cater for. The Earls of Northumberland and Westmoreland, the Percys and the Nevilles, joined him with their troops at Doncaster. As guardians of the Scottish border they had for a long time been accustomed to power and independence, and resented any interference from the distant king in London. The Percys were Lancastrians through allegiance to John of Gaunt (though Northumberland had quarrelled with him during the Peasants' Revolt) to whose power they probably owed the earldom. The son, Sir Henry Percy, nicknamed Hotspur, had been in Bolingbroke's retinue. He was then aged thirty-five, his father a venerable fifty-seven. The Nevilles had intermarried with the Percys, and Ralph Neville's wife, the Countess of Westmoreland, was Bolingbroke's sister.

These were good reasons for alignment, but the form the invasion anyway took was basically one of North versus South. With Lancaster, Northumberland and Westmoreland united, the Duke of York in the south-east was in a decidedly unconvincing position. Even there, where he might expect more support, there was marked reluctance on the part of the shire knights to turn out in arms against Henry and on behalf of Richard. No doubt they reasoned that if Gaunt's estates could be taken, nobody's property was safe. Moreover Richard's act, and Henry's grievance, raised the matter of justice. A rightful claim of inheritance was, among property-owners, a popular cause.

At the same time the towns and the burgesses had become fearful of more taxes, in the aftermath of the experience of *La Plesaunce*. Froissart records that the rumblings of unrest had been growing for some time, and he cited the Duke of Gloucester, shortly before his exile and death, as predicting civil disturbance. People would take no more. 'There will soon be serious trouble in this country. The people are beginning to grumble, and to say that they will stand this not much longer.' Richard's policy was in itself a recipe for civil war.

Bolingbroke's cause therefore united all possible influential support against Richard, and it marched under the banner of right, of justice and entitlement, and with the powerful backing of the sanctity of rights to property. With what would turn out to be a very characteristic sense of public relations, Henry made the most of these feelings. Firstly he claimed, and swore to Northumberland, that he wanted only his inheritance. He even

Bolingbroke takes his leave of the king of France after his period of exile. He was to sail from Boulogne to Ravenspur on the Humber while Richard was in Ireland.

said explicitly that he had no ambition for the Crown. Those following him were therefore not acting traitorously, and those refusing to aid Richard could feel that they remained loyal subjects. It was part of the knightly code that wrongs should always be put right, even if the wrongdoer was the king himself. These sentiments are very important to an understanding of how it was that Bolingbroke so easily swept to victory.

From Pontefract he issued letters, carefully playing on the goodwill he had already set up, and cultivating the distrust of Richard which he knew to exist. He told the citizens that the king planned further taxes. He told the Lords that the king was intending to back out of his French commitments to the extent of selling Gascony. He told the peasantry that Richard intended to keep them subjected. He even cast doubt on the legitimacy of Richard's title, by allowing an old rumour to be resurrected concerning a suppressed line from Henry III.

In view of all this it is very difficult to believe Henry when he claimed not to have come intending to acquire the throne. Even had he not set out from France with the intention, the total backing he received in the north and the ease of his progress southwards must have made him realize that such an ambition was realistic. As the temptation increased, his denial of it remained effective propaganda. There were many who would have hesitated to participate in deposing a king, had they known that that was what they were doing.

OPPOSITE This fifteenth-century manuscript illustration shows the judges and jury of the King's Bench. The independence and authority of the judiciary was well established by Richard's time, and we frequently find legal opinion being sought, even by kings. Richard himself appealed to the lawyers for a ruling on the attempt by the Lords Appellant to control the monarchy through a Commission of Government.

Richard's fleet was still at Waterford, his army dispersed in Leinster, and some further delay occurred before he could reassemble, march south, and embark. He landed at Milford Haven on about 25 July, but by then he had already sent the Earl of Salisbury, John de Montacute, to Conway in North Wales to raise support there and on the border. In the meantime, in his unfortunate absence, it had become apparent that he had virtually no support.

York and the Council had mobilized an army of sorts, and when Bolingbroke marched first south to Leicester, then turned abruptly west towards the Severn, the southern army moved in the same direction. It was clear that both were concerned with anticipating Richard's arrival, Bolingbroke to cut him off from London, York to join and protect him. Bristol was defended by the Council, who reached it first, York himself occupying

Berkeley Castle. His men, however, deserted to Bolingbroke's more powerful army, which arrived at about the same time as Richard reached Wales. The chronicler Walsingham, on whom we rely for parts of this story, says that York himself saw the justice of Henry's cause. He was, of course, Henry's uncle as much as he was Richard's. And insignificant as he was as a character, he may still have harboured thoughts of revenge for the death of his elder brother Thomas Woodstock, Duke of Gloucester, and for the confiscation of the lands of his other brother John of Gaunt. Edmund Langley, Duke of York, was then aged fifty-eight, and at this quite advanced age he took his one notable step and left his one mark on Britain's history. He abandoned Richard's cause and sided with Henry.

The city of Bristol surrendered without even the show of resistance. The townspeople opened the gates on 28 July, with the full consent of the Constable, Sir Peter Courtenay. Three of Richard's chamber-knights, including Bushy and Green, had taken refuge there, and they were handed over to Bolingbroke and summarily executed. Courtenay's act of apparent betrayal is curious, until one knows the background to it. He himself had been on the side of the Lords Appellant, having been appointed Chamberlain by them – and they of course included Bolingbroke – in place of Robert de Vere. The new revolution, then, can be explained partly in terms of the former one. Richard, on his return to power, had removed Sir Peter from the Chamberlainship, but had not moved him far enough. He made him Constable of Bristol, a lowly post for someone who had sat so high. Courtenay therefore had the motive of revenge.

By the time Richard was able to decide on his immediate action, Bristol had already fallen. With Bolingbroke at the Severn, he could not seek support in the south. He turned, as he always had done, to a territory he had reason to suppose loyal and reliable, that of the Cheshire border and North Wales. Salisbury was already there, and had begun to mobilize an army. The king therefore set off up the Welsh coast with a small company and little equipment to join the Earl in Conway. He left an army behind, but it was immediately weakened by desertion. His close friend the Duke of Albermarle, son of Edmund Langley, followed his father in desertion. Probably it was already becoming clear that defeat was likely. Richard left

OPPOSITE Richard's supporters are summarily executed by Bolingbroke's men.

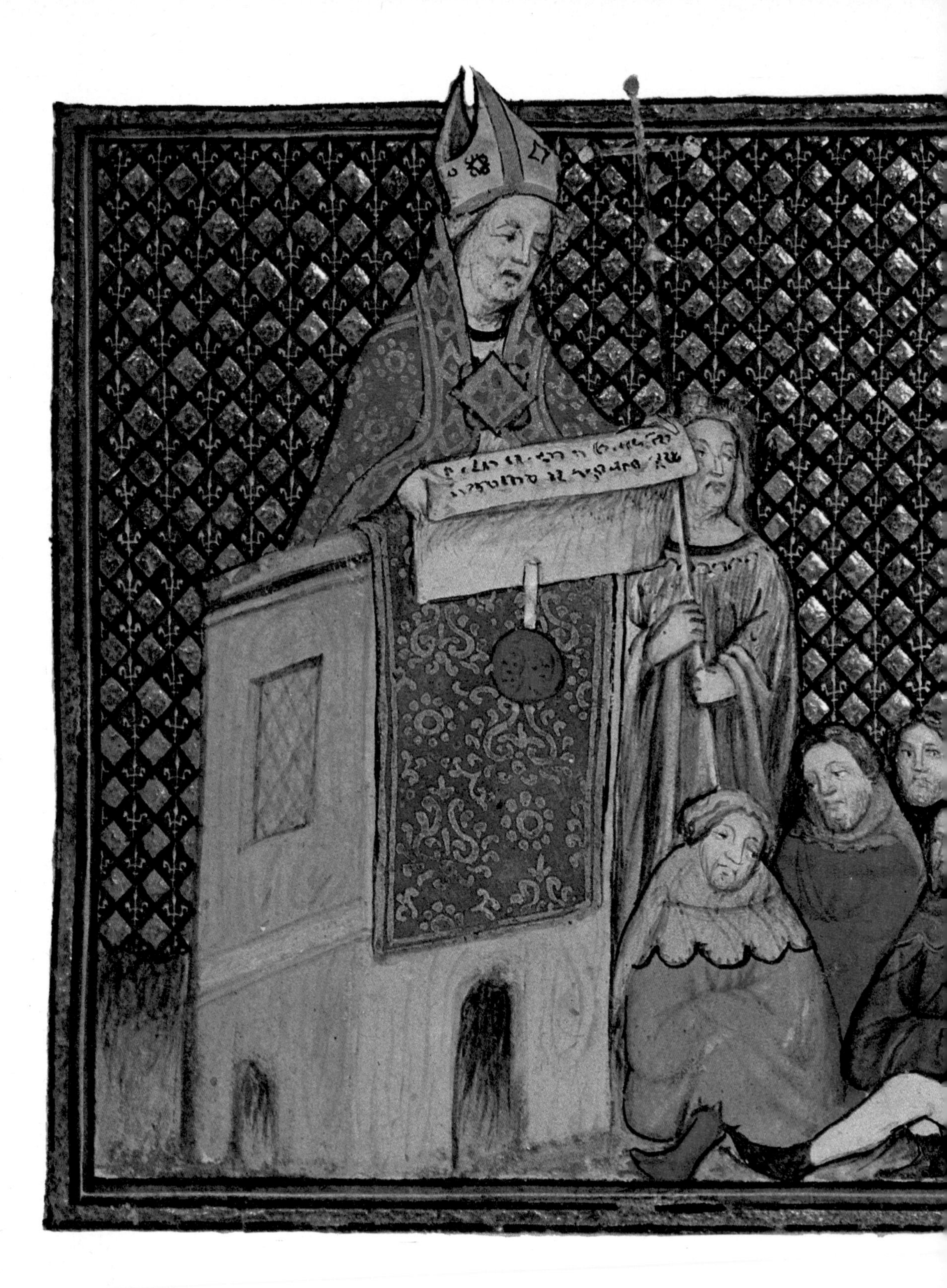

An early fifteenth-century French manuscript, showing Archbishop Arundel preaching in Bolingbroke's cause. Arundel, who had joined Bolingbroke in exile in Paris, returned with him and supported his campaign against Richard. He was reinstated by Henry, and presided at his coronation.

in charge of the southern army Thomas Percy, who would, had he stayed, have been subject to conflicting loyalties. But Percy too let him down, and when Richard had gone he allowed the army to disband.

Worse news still awaited him at Conway, where he had hoped to meet his salvation in the form of a Welsh and Cheshire army. Instead he found there only Salisbury himself with a small band of followers. The army had indeed been raised. But in the few weeks of uncertainty there had grown up rumours that the king was already dead, and the Earl had been unable to hold the men together. They had grown restless and dispersed.

Richard's intention was to make his base at Chester, but Bolingbroke, hearing of his movements, hurried north. He and his army rode into the king's most loyal territory as victorious conquerors. Adam of Usk, who was with them, tells of plunder and destruction. On 9 August, Henry reached Chester and executed the king's representative there. It was a few days later that Richard joined Salisbury in Conway, and probably in the hopes of restoring morale and persuading an army to reassemble he visited the other strong North Welsh castles of Beaumaris and Caernarvon during the next few days. The tour was fruitless, and he returned to the greater security and better provision of Conway.

Bolingbroke advanced some way towards his enemy, and sent ambassadors ahead. The Earl of Northumberland and the ex-Archbishop Arundel arrived with a small company of attendants in front of the impregnable walls of Conway, seeking an audience with the king. What Richard did not know, relying as he did on the security of his sanctuary in that strong Edwardian castle, was that they had left a considerable army only some six miles distant. Richard received the ambassadors, and the discussions lasted several days. It was about 13 August when Northumberland and Arundel arrived at Conway, and 19 August when they achieved their aim.

Shakespeare mistakenly sets this scene at Flint, distantly following the incorrect account by Froissart, in which Richard went straight to Flint Castle, not to Conway. Fortunately we have the first-hand account of the *Metrical History* by Jean Creton, who had been with Richard in Ireland, went ahead to Wales with Salisbury, and was to remain close to the king for

Henry Bolingbroke at Chester, having occupied Richard's most loyal territory, receives the Dukes of Exeter and Surrey. From an early fifteenth-century French manuscript.

the rest of the sad sequence of events. Creton said that Richard told his Council that he would have to agree to Northumberland's and Bolingbroke's demands, but that he regarded the agreement as a forced one and would not find it binding: 'If I can ever get him to my advantage, I will cause him to be foully put to death, just as he hath deserved.' The negotiations were in fact conducted in a spirit of duplicity on both sides.

Northumberland's message from Bolingbroke was to the effect that Henry's inheritance should be restored, that several of Richard's supporters should be given up to him, and that Parliament should be freed from royal control, with a post for Henry in the judiciary. In exchange he would make peace, and allow Richard to retain the Crown. The Council agreed, Northumberland waiting outside the room, to pretend to accept the terms. The Earl was called back in and informed. It was arranged that Richard should go to Flint to meet Henry, and Northumberland guaranteed him safe conduct. In spite of the fact that he had been sent with the specific task of extracting Richard from the safety of Conway and bringing him to Bolingbroke 'by reason or by craft', he went so far as to swear his good faith on the sacramental host: 'Each of them devoutly heard Mass; then the Earl, without further hesitation, made oath upon the Body of Our Lord.' That act of sacrilege and treachery in the chapel of Conway Castle must shock us still, and in the context of the codes and beliefs of the Middle Ages it would be hard to credit, were Creton not so specifically emphatic. The assumed impossibility of dissembling under such an oath must have been sufficient to tempt the wily Richard out of Conway's walls with only a handful of attendants.

They had agreed to break the journey at Rhuddlan Castle, a little over half-way to Flint, and by Richard's agreement the Earl rode ahead on the pretext of going to order the preparation of dinner. In fact he went no further than the place where he had hidden his army. Richard and about twenty of his men rode on in unaccustomed and innocent trust. About six miles from the bank of the river Conway the coastal path which they were following to Rhuddlan passes over the rocky and precipitous headland of Penmaenrhos. The rock, says Creton, was 'washed by the main sea', as indeed it still is. It was here that Richard was ambushed, as he passed over the narrow defile of the cliff path.

Richard received the Earl of Northumberland in Conway Castle, where
he had taken refuge. Northumberland had been sent by Bolingbroke
to lure Richard out of the safety of Conway, which he
did by swearing that Bolingbroke meant him no harm. This
however was a trick, as he had concealed an army nearby.

ABOVE Richard II is ambushed and captured by the Earl of Northumberland, who had concealed an army on his route along the North Wales coast. OPPOSITE ABOVE Richard had to pass across this rocky headland of Penmaenrhos, near the present town of Colwyn Bay, as he took the coastal path between Conway and Rhuddlan. 'We could not get away the other side owing to the rock', writes Jean Creton, who travelled with him. OPPOSITE BELOW Creton's eyewitness account mentions the rock 'washed by the main sea' at the point at which Richard was ambushed.

'We could not get away the other side owing to the rock, so cost what it might, we were forced either to die or pass into the midst of the Earl's people', Creton records.

Stow's *Annals*, quoted at the beginning of this book, written in the sixteenth century but closely based on good sources, give a graphic account of the confrontation. Richard knew 'well that he was betrayed by the Earle'. He thought of fleeing, but 'they would have caught him, ere he could have come to Conway.' The Earl pretended that the troops were for his safety, but he was not fooled. He told him 'it was contrary to his oth, for he had promised to have but sixe in his company and said therefore that he would goe back to Conwey', thus forcing Northumberland virtually to arrest him. They rode on to Rhuddlan to eat, and thence to Flint.

At Flint Henry treated Richard as his prisoner. He took him back to Chester the next day, and from there they rode to London. Creton tells us that Richard was treated humiliatingly, and Creton was there. An attempt was made by some Cheshire troops to rescue him, at some spot between Lichfield and Coventry, but it failed. The reign of Richard II was effectively over.

For the time being, however, Bolingbroke continued to treat him as king. Though he held him prisoner in the Tower, he had letters patent and writs to summon the new Parliament issued in Richard's name. As so often, we find to our surprise that it was felt necessary to support the power of might with the power of legality.

A committee was appointed, the first resort in any age of an English official in doubt as to what to do. Its task, like the task of so many subsequent committees, was to find a way of justifying a decision already taken. There was no doubt that Henry had now decided to become king. But he was a sufficiently careful politician to be anxious to do so with the law of the land behind him.

Significantly he was not eager to adopt the title by right of conquest. That indeed would have been to invite somebody to do the same to him. Moreover he was warned that it would lead to doubts about the safety of property – the very force which had brought him so successfully home – in that if the kingdom could be snatched in such a way, so could anything else. The

PREVIOUS PAGE Richard's abdication in the Tower of London. The official Lancastrian record was that he abdicated voluntarily, but his mood as described by Adam of Usk seems to have been bitter and resentful.

OPPOSITE Henry enters London, to cheers from the citizens. An illustration from a copy of Froissart's *Chronicles*.

committee found that Richard could be lawfully deposed 'by the authority of the clergy and people, on the grounds of having been guilty of 'perjuries, sacrileges, unnatural crimes, exactions from his subjects, reductions of his people to slavery, cowardice and weakness of rule'. The evidence is, to say the least, that these charges were an overstatement of Richard's crimes.

Henry had hoped that the committee would find that he had a valid hereditary title to the throne, but it was not so. They found no evidence for the lineage through his mother Blanche of Lancaster extending to an elder brother of Edward I, whose line, the legend said, had been put aside because of a deformity. Thus, though the lawyers obligingly permitted the deposition of Richard, they did not go so far as to offer Henry the peace of mind of rightful inheritance.

The assembly called in Richard's name met at Westminster Hall at the end of September. The day before, a deputation to Richard in the Tower had succeeded in getting his agreement to abdicate. Adam of Usk's description of Richard's mood at the time suggests that this would have been forced from him, rather than (as according to the official version) offered voluntarily: 'the King discoursed sorrowfully in these words, "My God! a wonderful land is this, and a fickle; which hath exiled, slain, destroyed, or ruined so many Kings, rulers and great men, and is ever tainted with strife and variance and envy . . ." '. One can easily recognize this as a source of Shakespeare's famous speech on the fate of kings. Usk says that he left the king 'musing on his ancient and wonted glory and on the fickle fortune of the world'.

The assembly accused Richard of having broken his coronation oath by ruling according to his own pleasure, rather than by law, thus clearly defining a precedent for a monarchy bound by constitutional restraints. It accused him of the full range of the unpopular acts which we have seen him undertake – the extortions, the rule through a personal rather than elected council, the extravagance, the shows of temperament, the murder of Gloucester and the revoking of the pardons. Henry then, with popular acclaim, proceeded to occupy the vacant throne.

He made two speeches, one before a sermon by the restored Archbishop, one after. Both were in English, and have been

OPPOSITE Richard's funeral, in an illustration from a British Museum manuscript. Richard was buried quietly at King's Langley, and only during the reign of Henry V was his body brought to Westminster Abbey, where it now lies.

recorded for us verbatim. In the first he made three claims to his right to the crown: he was descended of the royal line, he had achieved the throne by rightful conquest, and it had been necessary for him to do so in order to save the realm.

> . . . als I that am disendit be right lyne of the Blode Comyng fro the gude lorde kyng Henry therde and thorghe that right that God of his grace hath sent me, with helpe of my Kyn and of my Frendes to recover it; the which Rewme was in poynt to be undone, for defaut of Governance and undoyng of the gode Lawes.

He added after the sermon, and in qualification of one of his apparent claims, that he had no intention of extending his right of conquest as a principle:

> . . . it es noght my will that no man thynk that be waye of Conquest I wold disherit any man of his heritage, franaches, or other ryghtes, that hym oght to have, ne put hym out of that he had and has had by the gude lawes and customes of the Rewme; Except thos persons that has ben agan the gude purpose and the Commune profyte of the Rewme.

No one mentioned the claim of the young successor, then aged eight, to the Earl of March. A solitary voice, that of the Bishop of Carlisle, spoke up for Richard's rights. Like any common prisoner he had the natural right to speak in his own defence: '. . . it appears to me that you are about to give judgement, and to condemn King Richard, without hearing what he has to answer, or even his being present.' He dared to say that Bolingbroke was also in the wrong in returning illegally from exile, and demanded that King Richard (as he still called him) be brought 'to hear what he has to say, and to see whether he be willing to relinquish his crown to the Duke or not'.

. . . you are about to give judgement, and to condemn King Richard, without hearing what he has to say, or even his being present.

The assembly evidently did not dare to find the answer, which indicates that Richard's abdication was not the voluntary agreement that was officially claimed. The honest and courageous stand by Richard's friend was not only ignored, but summarily punished. He was imprisoned, and later deprived of his see. Henry was duly crowned by the hand of his close associate the Archbishop in Westminster Abbey on 13 October 1399.

Richard in the Tower took the news calmly. He remarked that 'he hopede that hys cosyn wolde be good Lord to hym'.

OPPOSITE Richard is imprisoned in the Tower of London. For the time being Henry continued to treat him as the king, and issued writs in his name.

The coronation of Henry IV, from Froissart's *Chronicles*.

The hope was temporarily fulfilled, in that he might well then have been brought to execution. Instead he was removed on 28 October to Leeds Castle in Kent, and from there taken north to secret imprisonment in Pickering, Knaresborough and eventually Henry's castle at Pontefract, in Yorkshire.

There he might have stayed in secluded retirement, but for a last flourish of hopeless resistance by his friends. York's son the Earl of Rutland (the same Duke of Albemarle who had deserted

Richard, now deprived of that title in a general reversal of earlier honours and gifts) may have been among the conspirators, and if so perhaps his part in it accounted for the failure of the plot. Henry appears to have been tipped off. He fled from Windsor Castle, where he was about to celebrate Christmas, shortly before the counter-revolutionaries stormed it. They also included the loyal Salisbury, Thomas Holland the Earl of Kent, and York's son-in-law Thomas Despenser, formerly the Earl of Gloucester. Henry was victorious thanks to widespread popular support; the rebels, pursued by his army, took refuge in Cirencester, but reckoned without the strength of feeling of the people of the town. Salisbury and Kent were executed by the citizens in the market square; Thomas Despenser fled, but was arrested and executed by the citizens of Bristol: Richard's antagonism of the burgess class sealed his downfall.

Henry at once carried out a purge. Some of Richard's more powerful supporters had been imprisoned in October, and others were now executed and hanged. In view of his bitter experience of the way in which Richard could restore himself from seeming defeat he knew it was now too dangerous to keep him alive. What precisely happened to him we do not know, and reports vary. A rumour even persisted for many years that he had escaped to Scotland, but it seems unlikely to be so. His body was brought slowly south to London, the face exposed for all to see, to be buried without ceremony at King's Langley; there it remained until the new sense of the throne's security at the start of the reign of Henry V permitted a general climate of reconciliation, when it was brought to Westminster Abbey to be reburied with due pageantry, to lie as it does now amongst his illustrious forbears.

In some accounts he had been suffocated, in others starved to death, while the official record claims he starved himself. Murdered or dead of grief, his own sad story ended sometime between the ninth and the seventeenth of February 1400 in the castle of Pontefract. He was thirty-three.

OVERLEAF Richard died at Pontefract, and his body was brought slowly south, his face exposed for all to see. Nevertheless the rumour persisted for some time that he had escaped and was still alive.

Edward' Tertius: reg 50
Richus Scdus reg 22

8 Bequest to History

IT IS an unavoidable fact that whatever I or any others may write, the image of Richard II that most people will retain, the image that will survive, is that conveyed by Shakespeare's play. How accurate an assessment is that? To what extent does *The Tragedie of King Richard the second* reflect the facts?

Shakespeare was not engaged in writing academic history but in striving to achieve an interpretation, within the scope of dramatic requirements, of what he regarded as historical fact. In some of his chronicle plays he shows confident artistic disregard for authenticity, and is prepared to manipulate character for dramatic effect. In *Richard II*, however, more than in most, he was working from reliable sources. He did his research meticulously, and the result is surprisingly close to what historians would accept as true.

The play opens with the high drama of the quarrel between Mowbray and Bolingbroke, the latter protesting his loyalty to the king. Gloucester's death, and Gaunt's suspicions of Richard, give extra tension to the situation of the court awaiting the crucial duel. At the last moment the king throws down his staff. The combatants are sentenced, Bolingbroke's term of exile shortened to placate Gaunt. Shortly after, however, the latter dies, and Richard, whose mind is set on his Irish wars, peremptorily commandeers his possessions. As Richard leaves for Ireland, Bolingbroke returns. The old Duke of York starts to muster an army, while Bolingbroke and Northumberland approach with their forces. But York, who has his own resentments against the king, is easily won over to Bolingbroke's side when they meet to parley. Salisbury is in Wales, the king still absent. Bristol falls, and Bushy and Green, among the few characters shown as genuinely loyal to Richard, suffer Bolingbroke's impetuous vengeance.

Richard then lands in Wales, joins Salisbury, but finds the Welsh army dispersed on the rumour of the king's death. He hears of the fall of Bristol, the execution of his men, the defection of York and the sweeping success of Bolingbroke's progress. He takes refuge in Flint Castle, where Northumberland comes as messenger from Bolingbroke intending to fetch Richard to talk terms with him, which he succeeds in doing. The king recognizes that he is outnumbered and already effectively deposed, and agrees to go with his cousin to London.

PREVIOUS PAGE Statues of Edward III, Richard II and Henry IV stand side by side in York Minster.

At an assembly in Westminster Hall Bolingbroke charges Richard's subordinates with Gloucester's death; on hearing that Richard agrees to his accession he determines to take the throne. The Bishop of Carlisle checks him with an outburst in Richard's defence, accusing Bolingbroke of treason, only to be arrested and charged himself.

Richard, however, is sent for, and relinquishes the crown. He is sent to the Tower, encountering the queen on the way, but orders arrive for him to be taken to 'Pomfret', her to France. In the meantime the Duke of York discovers that his son, 'Aumerle', is involved in a plot to kill the new king. He discloses the matter to Henry, who lets it be known that it would please him if Richard were dead. The ex-king, musing in melancholy in Pomfret Castle, is set upon by knights arrived to murder him. Bolingbroke, ordering vengeance on the rebels, receives with mixed feelings the proof of Richard's death, in the form of his corpse.

It will be seen from this bald summary that Shakespeare has been remarkably true to his sources, some of which are also ours, in telling the end of the story that we have surveyed in this book. Only in the apparent willingness of Richard to resign his throne do we find any indication of Lancastrian bias. It suited the dramatist's sense of tension to be fair to both sides, and the true moral ambiguity of much of Richard's behaviour comes over strongly. Above all Shakespeare was clearly fascinated, and understandably, by the character of the king himself.

Shakespeare's Richard is a man of moods. At the start of the play the dramatist displays Richard's self-conscious regality, which is to become so poignant a factor in his later decline. 'We were not born to sue, but to command ...' It is not entirely a likeable failing, but by making it so central a part of Richard's personality Shakespeare is true both to history and to the principle that tragedy arises from the destruction of a good man through an inherent weakness. His Richard is given to displays of sensitivity bordering on the sentimental. Arriving back in Britain he strokes the ground, and embarks on a long apostrophe to the earth of his kingdom – 'my gentle earth' – which is almost mawkish. Shakespeare well catches the sudden bursts of temper which the chroniclers, and the events, unanimously endorse: mistaking a message concerning the

OPPOSITE Shakespeare's tragedy of Richard II remains almost continuously in repertory. In this Prospect Theatre production of 1969 the king is played by Ian McKellen and his queen by Lucy Fleming.

LEFT Richard in one of Shakespeare's telling monologues. The Shakespearean image of Richard has much historical and psychological accuracy.

deaths of Bushy and Green for news of their desertion, he calls down terrible curses on them in what is evidently a scream of near-hysteria, only to sink into a deep depression when made to understand the truth. Even in the face of defeat he parades his regality immodestly, appealing, in the famous scene at Flint Castle, to the divine sanction bestowed by coronation. Shakespeare was probably more conscious than Richard could have been of the historical importance of the idea of the divine right of kings; but the claim is nevertheless in character. We believe him when he later says that he has difficulty shaking off the regal thoughts with which he has reigned. Bereft of kingship, he clings to the last to his habit of self-pity, and the introspection, which has throughout made him seem to be acting out an inner drama, is well expressed in the late scene in which he asks for a mirror and looks for signs of change in his own face. In his last scene he is philosophical and rational, though still highly-strung. And right at his end he displays the power of real physical action which must have been latent throughout the scenes of plaintiveness and anger. He seizes a battle-axe off the wall, and fells some of his assailants with it. Suddenly he is again the Black Prince's son, and the man who faced the peasants at Smithfield.

Shakespeare is true too to our understanding of Richard's physical appearance, referring to his paleness and his tendency to flush; and also to our knowledge of the political motivations of his court. When Aumerle says to him 'let's fight with gentle words, till time lend friends . . .' we see a situation made familiar by several of Richard's temporary peace-makings and their vengeful sequels.

It is, then, a fortunately accurate portrayal, and it is not surprising that it should be so. Shakespeare was, as so often, reworking existing material, in the shape of a play and a poem by other hands, but for his innovations he did his homework thoroughly. His immediate source was the chronicle of his contemporary Holinshed, who himself borrowed extensively from the chronicles of Hall, published in 1548. From this Shakespeare undoubtedly drew Richard's ambiguous character. It has been shown that he also studied Froissart, in the form of the translation by Lord Berners, and from this he gained not only one or two mistakes but a valuable insight into the role and imposing personality of John of Gaunt. There is also a French chronicle entitled *La Chronique de la Traïson et mort de Richard Deux, roy Dengleterre*, from which we get a fairer view of Richard's last phase than from the the chroniclers such as Walsingham and Froissart, who were understandably cautious not to contradict official Lancastrian versions of events. From the *Traïson* (as it is known) he drew his view of Richard's reaction to his defeat and downfall. Some authorities think that the dramatist also read Creton, but Creton was vehemently pro-Richard, and the generally Lancastrian view of the end and one or two errors of fact indicate that this is unlikely – though we must not discount possible dramatic reasons for such things as the location of the Conway scene, in amalgamation with the Flint events, at Flint Castle.

Let's fight with gentle words, till time lend friends.

Shakespeare's Bolingbroke was not fully developed as a character in this play, in which all other figures are simplified to form a context for the unravelling of Richard's problems. Shakespeare was to turn to him next, presenting in the two parts of *Henry* IV the determined but beleaguered person which his Bolingbroke, under the impetus of kingship, became. And history too shows us a well-intentioned man made wary and sad by the crown he had so hopefully accepted.

His reign had started with the hope of undoing the harm done by Richard; but Richard's problems were built into the times, and they had been only temporarily subdued by the usurpation. That too was to have its own problems, since the king could claim little right other than his popularity, and that, under the circumstances, was constantly in danger. Froissart rashly quotes a prophecy of Merlin to the effect that the crown would rest with the House of Lancaster. He had, he said, seen it come true. Sixty years later, with the accession of the Yorkist heir Edward IV, it was to come untrue again.

Henry did not intentionally begin his reign with a change of style. Indeed he adopted many of Richard's habits, keeping some of his close associates in office, and continuing to patronize the same writers and artists. It is in his relationship with the French that the main difference is apparent in the first years, hardly surprisingly in view of Richard's marriage and the policy which lay behind it. At first Henry acted peacefully enough. He allowed the widowed queen to return to France, in 1401; and he even sought to continue his predecessor's policy to the extent of requesting a French princess as a bride for his son. But it was all in vain: the court in France was still pro-Richard, and reluctant to recognize Henry as rightful king of England.

Henry, who knew French customs well, made use of French disunity to play one faction off against another, and it was as part of this scheme that he too undertook a French marriage, marrying Joan of Navarre in 1402. Meanwhile war had been re-opened in 1401, and Richard's peace, the major achievement of his reign, was over.

War (or hostility) with France entailed corresponding trouble with Scotland, and a new conflict likewise erupted there. Returning from Scotland in 1400 Henry found that a further difficulty had arisen in his troubled kingdom. Rebellion had broken out in Wales.

North Wales and the border country had always been, as we have seen, Richard's reserve of loyalty. There is no doubt that the success of the new revolt is partly to be attributed to the

A French manuscript illustration giving a fine topographical view of Paris *c.* 1400.

existence there of support for Richard. There were rumours that he was still alive, and it was still the intention of some people to reinstate him. Henry was to suffer all his reign from the illegitimacy of his accession. The revolt in Wales, however, was more widely based: there had been discontent, particularly among the peasantry, ever since the occupation of Wales by Edward I. Memories are long there, and Henry was to some extent the scapegoat for the high-handed policies of the Plantagenet invader.

As is so often the case the revolt was triggered by a seemingly small incident. Owain Glyndwr was a border squire, and in all respects likely to be loyal to Henry. He had served with Fitzalan, the Earl of Arundel, and possibly had been a squire to Bolingbroke himself. The matter flared up in the summer of 1400 after a quarrel between Glyndwr and Lord Grey of Ruthin over some land, which had the result that Grey, a friend of the king, managed to get Glyndwr outlawed. The latter then became the traitor he was accused of being, proclaimed himself Prince of Wales, and drew around him all the latent nationalistic hostility to the English Crown.

The local revolt spread quickly, and the rebels met the new king and his forces in a pitched battle at Welshpool. In 1401 Prince Henry (later Henry V) was sent to Chester with Hotspur, Northumberland's son, to counter-campaign in North Wales. But it was shortly after that movement that a surprising and significant event took place. The Percys changed sides. Having been largely responsible for placing Henry on the throne, they now sought to remove him. Perhaps it had never been their intention that he should become king. Perhaps they had all along been seeking to improve their own position of power at the expense of the throne. Perhaps they had only supported him because they believed his oath that he had no ambitions for the Crown. Or alternatively things might subsequently have changed: perhaps they had been disillusioned by his lack of support for their border interests.

These events are of interest to us now for the evidence they give that the issue between Richard and Henry was by no means clear-cut. The new king had, it suddenly appeared, as little support in the national power-structure as the old one before him. Neither the people nor the great barons would offer him unconditional loyalty. With Wales, Scotland and now Northumberland against him, his hold on Britain seemed suddenly tenuous. It was only to be expected that the French would then join with the rebels.

Richard's supposed successor (if he were indeed dead) was Edmund Mortimer, heir to the earldom of March and hence a descendant of Edward III's second son and, in the complexity of that dynasty, the Yorkist heir. In 1402 he was captured by Glyndwr's troops. He was at the time eleven years old, and his youth had probably been the main factor in the absence of any claim on his behalf when Henry usurped the throne. Glyndwr made much of the fact that Mortimer was Richard's valid heir, and no doubt with little difficulty persuaded his young captive to pursue his own ends through Glyndwr's successes. Mortimer, at all events, sided with the revolt, to the extent of marrying Owain's daughter. Alliance by marriage encircled Henry: Northumberland's son Hotspur was married to Mortimer's sister.

Glyndwr's treaty with the French was made as prince of the independent country of Wales in 1404, and had this then been followed by the arrival of the support which France offered, Henry's reign might suddenly have been over, four years after it had begun. In 1403, however, the rebels had suffered a temporary set-back, which was to be the first symptom of their eventual incapacity. Hotspur was killed that July at a battle near Shrewsbury, an event which left the Percys further alienated from the Crown, but which proved the king's military strength.

One result of the battle of Shrewsbury was the courageous but extreme measure of the 'Tripartite Indenture'. Britain, the rebel leaders decided, was to become several separate provinces. Glyndwr was to rule Wales, Northumberland the north, and Mortimer the rest of the country. Had the French fleet which was supposedly arriving to implement this scheme actually reached shore, our national history might have been significantly different. But for some reason it failed to land. Prince Henry was successfully campaigning in Wales, and Owain's support dwindled with the natural acceleration which sets in once desertion starts. Northumberland died fighting the Scots. Glyndwr's family were captured on the fall of Harlech Castle in

1409. Mortimer had, in the meantime, died. In 1410 battles in Shropshire finished the war, and gave some security to Henry's crown for the first time in his reign.

Henry IV reigned over Britain for another three years, dying at the age of forty-six, broken in health and spirit, on 20 March 1413. It was the fact of his reign, rather than any events of it, that had the greatest impact on British history. The act of deposing Richard left a permanent line of claimants threatening the Lancastrian throne. If Henry wished that his claim to right of descent had been clearer, his successors came to wish that even more. The Wars of the Roses, in which the Houses of York and Lancaster tore Britain apart in their struggle for the throne, form one of the bloodier and more destructive of the phases of our history. The ghost of the murdered Richard might have taken some satisfaction from the eventual outcome of his betrayal.

We have seen throughout that in the Middle Ages might did not equal right. Possession was not a sufficient guarantee of ownership of the Crown or any other title. Acts had to be just, or at least justified. That was Henry's weakness, and the obstacle to the success of the House of Lancaster as a dynasty. Two more generations, two more Henrys, were to complete it. When eventually another Henry, Henry Tudor, with his success of the Battle of Bosworth in 1485, brought to an end the long conflict and to a great extent the Middle Ages in Britain, ushering in a new age and a new stability, he then consolidated his basically Lancastrian claim to the throne by marriage to the Yorkist heiress. But by then Britain had learnt, through bitter experience, a more realistic attitude to the finer points of pedigree. The country wanted peace and a strong monarchy.

The effect of Richard's mistakes was to set back the development of Britain's particular achievement, the English Renaissance, but probably the set-back itself brought the benefit that when it came it did so into a world better suited to receive it. There was a time during Richard's reign when it seemed that Britain was about to move into just such an age as the Battle of Bosworth permitted, with national interests and those of the Crown united, the priorities being peace, prosperity, and the cultivation of social progress, commerce, and the arts. Much of the style of Richard's government anticipated the achievements

OPPOSITE The uprising of Owain Glyndwr (anglicized by Shakespeare as Owen Glendower) started as a private quarrel but quickly spread to become a national war. It demonstrated the basic disunity of the country and the insecurity of the Crown at the start of the reign of Henry IV.

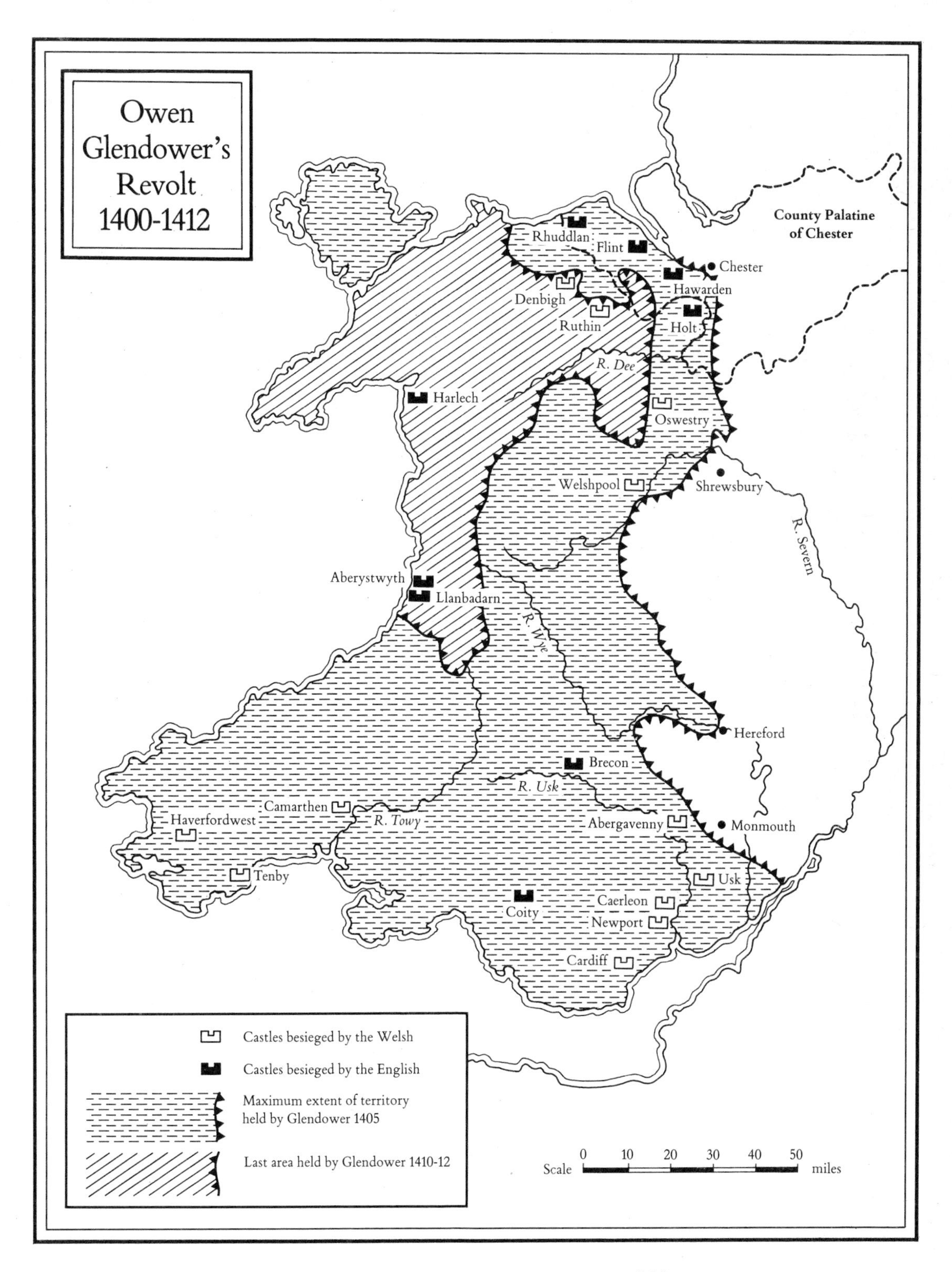
Owen Glendower's Revolt 1400-1412
County Palatine of Chester
Rhuddlan
Flint
Chester
Hawarden
Denbigh
Ruthin
Holt
R. Dee
Harlech
Oswestry
Welshpool
Shrewsbury
R. Severn
Aberystwyth
Llanbadarn
R. Wye
Hereford
Brecon
R. Usk
Camarthen
Haverfordwest
R. Towy
Abergavenny
Monmouth
Tenby
Usk
Caerleon
Coity
Newport
Cardiff
Castles besieged by the Welsh
Castles besieged by the English
Maximum extent of territory held by Glendower 1405
Last area held by Glendower 1410-12
Scale 0 10 20 30 40 50 miles

The effigies of Henry IV and his queen, Joan of Navarre, in Canterbury Cathedral. Henry aged fast and deteriorated in health and spirit under the strain of a troublesome reign.

of the Tudors and Stuarts. Unfortunately the difficulties they faced were faced to a greater extent by Richard, and in his time the means of dealing with them had not sufficiently developed. The power of Parliament and the constitutional nature of the monarchy grew in prominence after his death, and it was those factors, perhaps, which allowed the growth of a more realistic arrangement.

But the fact remains that for a time, and a crucial one, Richard raised his country to a level of cultural and political achievement which had not occurred before, and which was not to occur again until the English Renaissance. Had this peace lasted, and had he lived, a climax of British history might then have been achieved. For a few years it seemed almost a possible horizon. History had another valley to negotiate, and the summit Richard thought himself to be on turned out to be a false one. Probably an over-estimation of his position then contributed to his undoing. In judging Richard we should not forget the euphoric effect of the view from that high ridge.

Chronology

1367 Birth of Richard Plantagenet to Edward, the Black Prince, and Joan, the Fair Maid of Kent.

1376 Death of the Black Prince.

1377 Edward III died and Richard succeeded to the throne. John of Gaunt's faction in control of Parliament.

1377–84 John Wyclif preached Lollardy.

1380 William of Wykeham's New College, Oxford, founded.

1381 John Ball and Wat Tyler led the Peasants' Revolt. Murder of Archbishop Simon Sudbury.

1382 Richard II's marriage to Anne of Bohemia.

1388 The crisis of the Lords Appellant and the Merciless Parliament.

1394 Death of Anne of Bohemia.
Richard II left for Ireland.

1395 Lollard Movement came to a head.

1396 Marriage of Richard II to Isabelle, daughter of Charles VI of France, cementing the truce established by Richard in the Hundred Years War.

1398 Court of Chivalry: quarrel between Henry Bolingbroke and Thomas Mowbray. Their subsequent exile.

1399 Death of John of Gaunt.
Richard II sailed to Ireland. Bolingbroke returned from France and gathered troops in the north. Richard ambushed and deposed. He was imprisoned in the Tower.
Bolingbroke was crowned Henry IV.

1400 Death of Richard II at Pontefract Castle.

HOUSES OF YORK AND LANCASTER

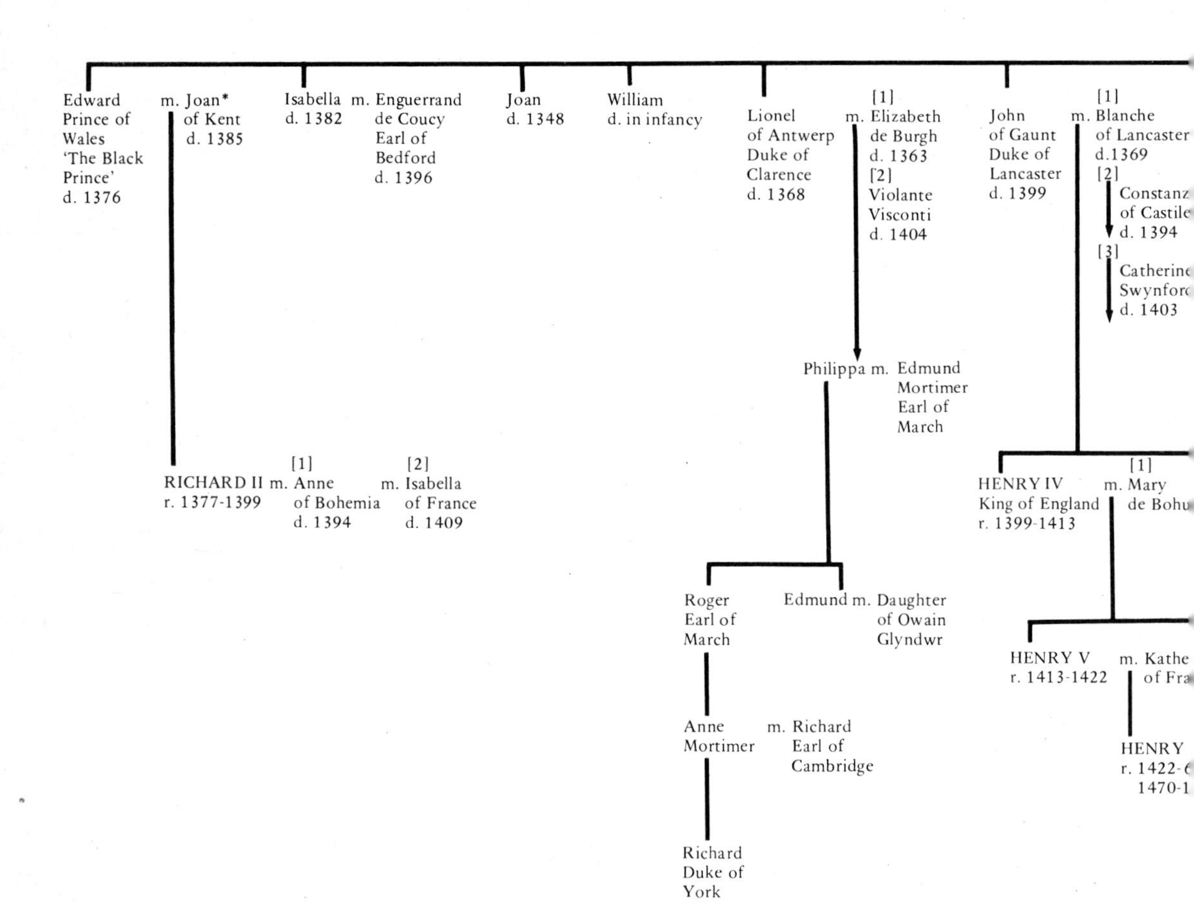

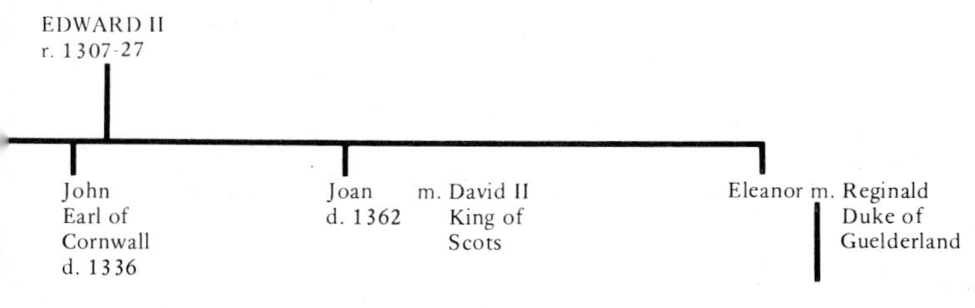

EDWARD II
r. 1307-27
John
Earl of
Cornwall
d. 1336
Joan
d. 1362
m. David II
King of
Scots
Eleanor m. Reginald
Duke of
Guelderland

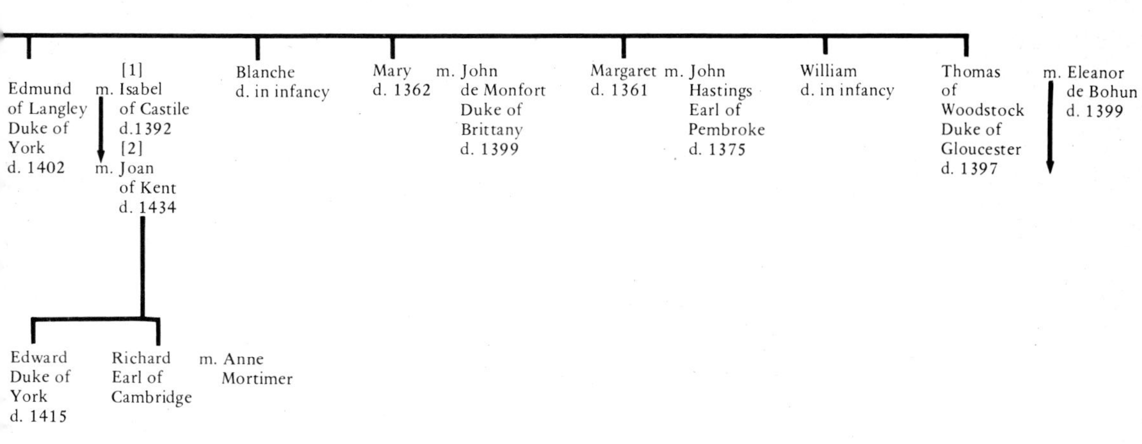

Edmund
of Langley
Duke of
York
d. 1402
[1]
m. Isabel
of Castile
d.1392
[2]
m. Joan
of Kent
d. 1434
Blanche
d. in infancy
Mary
d. 1362
m. John
de Monfort
Duke of
Brittany
d. 1399
Margaret
d. 1361
m. John
Hastings
Earl of
Pembroke
d. 1375
William
d. in infancy
Thomas
of
Woodstock
Duke of
Gloucester
d. 1397
m. Eleanor
de Bohun
d. 1399
Edward
Duke of
York
d. 1415
Richard
Earl of
Cambridge
m. Anne
Mortimer

Other issue

Select bibliography

The most accessible works covering the reign of Richard II are as follows:

Goodman, Anthony, *A History of England from Edward II to James I* (Longman, 1977)
Hutchinson, H. F., *The Hollow Crown: a life of Richard II* (Methuen, 1979)
Mathew, Gervase, *The Court of Richard II* (John Murray, 1968)
Tuck, A., *Richard II and the English Nobility* (Edward Arnold, 1973)

Other works concerned with the period of Richard's life and reign:

Barton, John and Joy Law, *The Hollow Crown* (Hamish Hamilton, 1971)
Brewer, Derek, *Chaucer in his Time* (Longman, 1973)
Brewer, Derek, *Chaucer and his World* (Eyre Methuen, 1978)
Burke, John, *Life in the Castle in Medieval England* (Batsford, 1978)
Cowie, Leonard W., *The Black Death and the Peasants Revolt* (Wayland, 1972)
Richards, Denis and Arnold D. Ellis, *Medieval Britain* (Longman, 1973)
Trevelyan, G. M., *Illustrated English Social History*, Volume One, *Chaucer's England and the Early Tudors* (Longman, 1942)

The relevant works of Froissart, Chaucer and Langland, and the romance *Sir Gawain and the Green Knight* are all available in Penguin Classics.

Index